*We dedicate this book to the amazing wives God has given us:*
*Soreya Thyne and Kathy Hunt. Thank you for patiently supporting us*
*as we invested the time and resources to make this book a reality.*
*We also recognize that we talked about accountability way more than a*
*wife should have to listen to any topic, and that you supported us as we*
*applied and practiced this in our lives each day.*

*We are blessed to be loved by such beauties*
*and thankful to have you by our side.*

# CONTENTS

# FOREWORD

When Salem Thyne and Robert Hunt first began talking about accountability, it was anchored in a business context, as part of a discussion within Renaissance Executive Forums, the CEO peer group Robert leads in Dallas, designed to equip leaders to achieve their personal and professional goals.

Salem showed Robert the well-known "Accountability Ladder" graphic, and this sparked an ongoing conversation about how accountability affects all areas, not simply for leaders or organizations, but for families, schools, and communities. Too often, Robert and Salem lamented, individuals fail to recognize that the power to effect positive change can begin by accepting responsibility—by becoming accountable.

This book is the result of their intensive exploration of the stages of accountability, the step-by-step navigation that can transform victims into victors. Robert and Salem speak with authenticity of the challenges they've faced and the changes they've made, personally and professionally, to become more accountable in all areas of life.

In this book, they coach readers in this journey, equipping them with the skills and knowledge to take control of their thoughts, actions, and behaviors in order to become truly accountable in their relationships, their decision making, their work, and how they choose to live.

Salem and Robert's goals for this book are clear:

- Impact and change lives, including ours

- Open people's minds to the potential of living victoriously

- Empower leaders to free their teams

- Help people who are struggling to make this climb on their own

This is a book for every reader who wants to push past long-held limitations and obstacles, for employers to share with their employees, and for parents to share with teens—for everyone who wants a better life.

Every day, you have the opportunity to make a choice. You can choose to take responsibility for yourself and your life going forward; or you can rely on excuses, blaming others, saying you can't, and waiting for change to happen to you. You can choose to be a victim or a victor.

Robert Hunt and Salem Thyne want to equip you to become accountable—to acknowledge reality, accept responsibility, and move toward your goals with fresh energy and enthusiasm. In this book, they explain how. With a message that is clear, inspiring, and motivating, they help you navigate through each stage of the journey from victim to victor, identifying how to overcome obstacles and sharing strategies and tips, key resources you can rely on when facing setbacks and challenges. They explain the transition from lack of awareness to acknowledging your reality, accepting the past without letting it write your future story.

This is an empowering book, full of Robert and Salem's honesty, transparency, trademark humor, and plenty of tough love. They have seen the impact accountability has had on their lives. They've used these principles with family members, with colleagues, and as leaders in their own organizations. Now, they want to see their message of the power of personal accountability spread—to help others lead a better life, a rich and full and motivated life.

> *"Most people are ignorant of the accountability life requires us to have. They have become comfortable being a victim and don't even know that there is a better way. We want people to stop blaming others and live a life full of peace and joy as they face the challenges of life. We want them to see that they can be victorious."*

# INTRODUCTION

## This Is Accountability

You made a choice when you picked up this book. Whatever attracted you to the subject matter, whatever called to you and said, "Hey, read *this*," it was a first step on a journey that could take you somewhere better than where you are right now. In fact, no matter where that happens to be, we can almost guarantee your life will be better if you read this book. It has been for us!

The key word there being *if*. That's kind of what accountability is all about.

But before we get into that, we should let you know who we are and why we think we're qualified to talk about this subject. We're Salem Thyne and Robert Hunt—husbands, dads, business leaders, and transplants from Southern California to the Dallas/Fort Worth area of Texas. Robert is the owner of Renaissance Executive Forums Dallas, an international CEO peer group designed to equip business leaders to achieve their personal and professional goals—which, to put it a little more simply, means he brings business leaders together to help each other be their best. Salem is a member of that group and the CEO of Fort Worth–based oil and gas firm Engineered Salinity. So those are our day jobs.

Our obsession with accountability started when Salem showed Robert the "Accountability Ladder" graphic from the book *The Oz Principle,* by Craig Hickman, Roger Connors, and Tom Smith. The ladder is a popular tool in the business world that helps managers diagnose and deal with accountability issues among their employees by determining where they fall on an imaginary ladder. The ladder itself is a scale that starts at complete cluelessness and reaches all the way up to total accountability.

We initially started talking about the accountability ladder in a business context, and as the application of these principles took off, we realized that accountability doesn't end at 6:00 p.m. or whenever you get off work. Accountability, and conversely a lack of accountability, impacts *all* areas—not just leaders or organizations but families, schools, communities, governments, and the entire world. All too often our problems can be traced to the simple fact that most people don't know that the power to effect positive change in any of these (or other) areas can begin simply by accepting responsibility—by becoming accountable. And everyone, including you, has that superpower.

That's why we wrote this book.

## The Accountability Mountain

When we took accountability out of a strictly business context and applied it to other areas of life, it became clear that the journey to real accountability is less like a ladder and more like a mountain. After you climb out of the muck of ignorance and blame and begin to accept your reality and become accountable, you have some options. Once you pass the point where you're able to accept your reality, it's easy and acceptable to reach a level where you're comfortable and stay there. You can't really do that with a ladder, which is basically designed to move you straight up (or down) and keep you constantly climbing until you reach the top. There aren't many spots where it's comfortable to stop and rest. With a mountain, the climb is more gradual. You can take time to stop and enjoy the view, think about where you might want to go next, or replenish your energy before moving on.

And you don't need to go all the way to the summit—reaching a lower peak may be all you want or need. Although once you experience the power of accountability in your own life, we're willing to bet you will press on to the top.

We know this because we've seen the impact accountability has had on our lives and the lives of the people around us. That's why we're so passionate about this topic. We used the same principles we're going to explore in this book with ourselves, with family members, and with colleagues, as leaders in our organizations as well as in our day-to-day lives. And the impact has been incredible. So now that we've passed the R&D phase, we're ready to share the message of the power of peak accountability with the world and with you, as well as a path to get up that metaphorical mountain. We truly believe it will help you lead a better life—a rich, full, and motivated life.

Which all sounds awesome … but also begs the question, "What exactly *is* accountability?"

# You Own It

In our minds, accountability comes down to these three words. *You own it.* There are fancier, longer definitions, but we think this sums it up beautifully. Late for a meeting? You own it. Missed your credit card payment? You own that too. There's no the-dog-ate-my-homework-traffic-was-a-nightmare-my-mother-didn't-love-me BS. There's also no that's-not-fair-nobody-told-me-it's-not-my-job or any of that head trash. It's on you. You did it or you didn't do it. You are responsible. There's no one else to point a finger at but you. Why? Because you own it.

We may all come from different circumstances, but regardless of where you start in life or what you bring to the table, ultimately what happens next is determined by your choices. For example, imagine you're in a situation where you really, really need money, as quickly as possible. You can

a. go knock over a liquor store, or

b. hustle and ask everyone you know if there's any work in or outside your field that anyone they know might hire you to do.

Both of these options will lead to the same result—money in your pocket. But if you choose to rob a liquor store (or cheat on your spouse, or lie to your boss), you can't ever say it didn't happen. You can't reset it. You can't erase it. There's no going back in time. You own it.

*Once you make a choice in your life, you will automatically face consequences, whatever they might be.*

That's the key to accountability—understanding that the decisions you make have consequences. You have to either be able to accept those consequences and all that they entail or take a path that guarantees you won't have to. However, there's a silver lining to the momentary pain that comes with owning it. When you own a problem, you can actually fix the problem. For example, if you chose option (b) in the example above, the extra work might help you solve your money problems in the short term and then the long term.

> *That's the key to accountability—understanding that the decisions you make have consequences.*

The point is that ultimately, you are in control of your own life, success, happiness, health, and peace—not your boss or your teacher or the government or the system. That's something we're not told and we're not taught anymore, maybe because the institutions that used to teach us what account-ability meant, like church every Sunday or scouting after school or workplaces where you spent your entire career, are less common in modern life. But—and this is going to be a theme you'll see a lot in this book—"Who cares?"

Yes, our lives are more fragmented. Yes, the traditional structures that used to provide a framework may have less influence over society at large. But forgive us if we have kumquats for brains, but so what? Your church can't make you happy. Your job can't make you happy (or unhappy, for that matter). Maybe they can provide some tools and show you how to use them. But ultimately, no one can control your happiness except you. Because no one can hold you accountable but you.

# Salem's Lot

Salem was first introduced to the concept of accountability when he was a senior in high school, courtesy of his AP English teacher. Back then, Salem was one of those kids who thought he knew more than everybody else because he was seventeen and super smart. He didn't need to work hard to get through school, so he spent the entire first half of his senior year screwing around, challenging his teacher on assignments, and fighting her about every little thing, just to mess with her. It wasn't that he didn't know he needed that credit to graduate high school; it was more that, because he was a super-smart kid, there was no doubt in his mind that he would get it.

Still, at some point it must have dawned on Salem that he might be cutting it close. But he figured, "So what if I kind of dug myself a hole? She'll let me do a whole bunch of extra assignments on the back end and dig my way out." So Salem reached an agreement with his teacher to do just that. Or something like an agreement. At least Salem *thought* she'd do it. Because why wouldn't she? He was, after all, super smart. He *deserved* to graduate.

By graduation day, Salem had done a pile of extra assignments and term papers nobody else did (to make up for the fact that he didn't do all the work that everybody else did earlier in the year). As long as he aced his final, he was confident he would get a free pass and slide through, and everything would be fine.

Graduation day in Bakersfield, California, where Salem is from, is kind of a goof-off day. Nobody really goes to school; they just hang out and play volleyball with their friends. But Salem must have had some kind of feeling, because he went into the school real quick, just to make sure he'd done well on his AP English final. His teacher delivered the good news: "Yeah, you got an A—you aced your final. Great job." Mission accomplished. Salem went back to the volleyball game and then home to get ready for graduation that night.

At about four o'clock in the afternoon, Salem's father, who also happens to be super smart, with a PhD to prove it, called him over. "Hey," he said, "I got a call from your school."

"Oh," said Salem. "What did they want?"

His dad looked at him. "You're not graduating."

Oh, crap.

Then he said, "I don't think I can say anything more to you that's going to make you feel more upset than you are now." (Something Salem was very grateful for at the time.)

But ultimately, his dad was right. Salem was devastated, shocked, humiliated, a little confused, and really, really angry … all at the same time. His teacher had told him it would be okay! Or at least she'd let him think it would. He went through all the possible reasons why this life-altering catastrophe had befallen him.

The teacher was a (w)itch. The system was unfair. Actually, *life* was unfair. The head trash was piling up fast and furious, and his brain was starting to swim.

A friend's mother somehow convinced him to go to graduation anyway, so he did. And when he showed up, it was obvious that the decision to deny him his diploma had been made on very short notice. Because sitting in the middle of all his classmates up on the stage was a single empty chair. A chair with his name on it. Right next to Linh Tran (a name that still haunts Salem to this day, thirty years later).

Salem sat down in the auditorium and looked at all his friends up on stage. He stared at the empty seat next to Linh Tran where he should have been sitting. And he felt like crap.

For the first time in his life, Salem was experiencing *consequences* for the actions he had taken and the things he had done. And in that moment, watching all his friends and Linh Tran move into the next phase of their lives, he also realized … he had a choice.

He could blame everything on everyone else and be pissed off and accept the life of a loser and a failure and a high school dropout. Or maybe he could do what some of his friends were suggesting and file a grievance, or challenge the school board, or ask his parents to intervene on his behalf.

But there was also a third option that, for some reason, held some appeal. He could actually accept the consequences of his actions. He could own it. And that's what Salem chose to do. He went on to complete his education and was a shining star in the Nuclear Navy Program, and he became a confident leader in the business world.

That was Salem's first experience with accountability. It wouldn't be his last … but it was a good place to start.

\* \* \*

We shared this story for a reason. We were all that kid once. Robert was definitely that kid, as you will learn in chapter 1. Maybe, in some ways, you're still that kid now. And, hey, that's perfectly fine. No judgment here. Because you're here now. The only thing that matters is what happens next. None of us is born accountable, and we've never met anyone who is accountable *all* the time. Accountability is a choice you can make every single day, in big moments and small ones. There's always going to be another opportunity to choose to take responsibility for yourself and your life as opposed to relying on excuses, blaming others, and/or waiting for change to happen to you. You get to choose to be a victim or a victor. There's more power in that than you can possibly imagine.

The path to peak accountability is a journey that is never over. The two of us are constantly pushing ourselves to be more and more accountable—just when we think we've reached the summit, we realize that we can still do more, we can still be better. It's more like a state of mind you adopt rather than a place that you reach and the journey ends. However, you don't have to get that far up the mountain to start reaping the rewards of facing your life and yourself more honestly. Accountability is a skill you can practice and learn, like a muscle you can develop. The more you practice it, the more it works, the easier it gets, and the better your results get.

*Accountability is a skill you can practice and learn, like a muscle you can develop. The more you practice it, the more it works, the easier it gets, and the better your results get.*

Most people don't know this. Most people are basically ignorant of the accountability we should (and can) all take on in life. We certainly were when we started this journey. It's easy to get comfortable being a victim, and you'll certainly have plenty of company there. Because most people don't know that there is a better way. We wrote this book because we want people to know how transformative it is when you stop blaming other people and own it. It's possible to live a life full of peace and joy while facing the challenges life brings.

In other words, instead of being a victim, you can be victorious. Instead of life leading you, you can lead your life.

# How to Use This Book

We designed this book to give you the tools that will equip you for that victory, regardless of where you are in life right now. We'll start out at the very bottom of the mountain and work our way up to acknowledging reality, accepting responsibility, and finally moving toward your goals with fresh energy and enthusiasm. At each stage of the journey from victim to victor, we'll help you understand the lay of the land, identify the obstacles you're likely to face, and share strategies, tips, and key resources you can rely on when facing setbacks and challenges. We'll also share tools to help you master each stage of the Accountability Mountain.

Together, we'll climb the path from lacking awareness to acknowledging your reality, accepting the past without letting it write your future story. Along the way, we'll share some of the challenges we've faced and the changes we've made, personally and professionally, to become more accountable in all areas of our lives. And we'll coach you through your own journey, equipping you with the skills and knowledge you need at each step to take control of your actions and behaviors in order to become truly accountable in yourself, your work, and your life. The results will transform your relationships, your

# PART I

## The View From Below

Like we said, we're starting this journey at the very beginning—at the bottom of the mountain. Down here, you're as far from accountability as you can possibly be. The peak is so far up in the clouds that you can't even see it, especially since, down where you are, the view is obscured by all the muck and head trash that's been clouding your perceptions. You don't know what's up there above you, and whatever it is, it feels scary and unsafe. You're pretty sure you probably can't handle it. Which is why you stay where you are, even if it sucks.

This is the perspective of a victim. Complete, total, utter powerlessness.

But while the trail ahead might look like an impossible climb, especially since you can't see where you're going, remember the old adage: a journey of a thousand miles begins with a single step. This first half of the book will be dedicated to getting you, single step by single step, past the muck and up above the head trash that clouds your vision. Slowly but surely, you'll climb out of the fog of obliviousness and blame and excuses and into the clean, clear light of accountability. Beginning on the very next page.

# CHAPTER ONE

## Mountain? What Mountain?

*Nobody can hold anyone accountable. We can only do that for ourselves. However, we can be bold and honest with people in our lives so they wake up and see the opportunity for a better life if they choose the power of peak accountability.*

—**ROBERT HUNT**

Robert's first experience with accountability came when he was just entering adulthood—around the same age Salem was when he experienced the story we told in the introduction. Unlike Salem, however, he had managed to make it out of high school with a diploma and was now in his first semester of college at California State University, Fullerton. The school was right in his hometown, and because there was a major state university so close to home, a lot of kids from his high school went there, including a lot of Robert's buddies.

Going to college with the same people he'd hung out with in high school made college feel almost like an extension of high school. The campus was different, the teachers were different, the classes were different, but Robert and his buddies were the same. They basically treated college like high school—that is, not especially seriously. They goofed off. They talked in class. Just like they always had.

Then one day in one of his classes, Robert and his buddies were goofing off as usual, and the professor asked them to quiet down. Maybe they didn't hear him, or maybe they just didn't take him seriously, but they kept doing whatever they were doing, and the next thing they heard was the professor snapping, "That's it! You guys, get out!"

That got their attention. They stopped and looked at the teacher, who repeated, "Get out of my class!" So they got out, went out into the courtyard and hung out, and didn't really give the whole incident much more thought.

That was on a Tuesday.

On Thursday, which was the next day the class met, Robert went back as usual and took his seat. The professor looked at him and said, "I thought I told you to get out of my class." Robert was confused. Hadn't that already happened? "I kicked you out," the teacher explained. Robert's response?

"That was Tuesday."

The professor looked at him and said, "Boy, this is *college*. When you're kicked out, you're kicked out." Robert just stared at him. "Nobody cares if you go to college!" the professor went on, exasperated. "I don't care. Your parents don't care. You want to go to college, go to college. You don't, don't go. But *don't* be in my class!"

Robert had been caught completely off guard. It was humiliating. He looked like a complete idiot in front of everyone. Nobody had ever told him that if he mouthed off in class, he could be permanently kicked out. Just like nobody'd ever told Salem that if he blew off half of his AP English work, he might not graduate.

He was trapped at the bottom of the mountain, at the very, very lowest stage of accountability—lack of awareness.

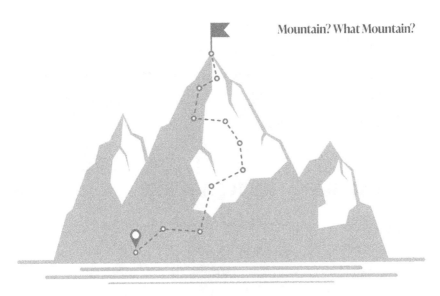

# You Are Here

When you're at the Lack of Awareness stage of the journey, you don't even know there is a mountain to climb (hence the title of this chapter). You have little to no idea where you are or how you got there, let alone how you can possibly get out. You live your life doing what you think you have to do, because what choice do you have? You're stuck, and you feel you have no power to change it. You're a victim—of circumstances, of your own lack of understanding … of life, basically.

This is the "nobody told me" phase of accountability. Or the "I didn't know" phase. When you have an "accountability moment" like Robert did in this phase, your responses are usually about your obliviousness to the situation that "caused" your problem. How can it be your fault if you didn't know about it in the first place?

As you've gone through life, you've probably discovered a lot of things "nobody told you." But the reality is that somebody probably did tell you at some point. It's not like nobody ever told Robert that his actions might have consequences. It's just that he hadn't experienced those consequences until that Thursday in his college class. That's what made it matter. Experiencing the consequences made it real. So Robert wasn't oblivious to the fact that he shouldn't talk in class. He was oblivious to the fact that our actions, including talking in class, have consequences.

## Accountability Then and Now

It's kind of ironic that we each had our first brush with accountability just as we were leaving childhood and entering adulthood. It says something about the way we as a society are raising our children. Had we faced any sort of meaningful consequences for our behavior before it really mattered, we might have learned those particular lessons earlier. However, as a society, we've successfully removed a lot of the consequences from our lives.

Two hundred years ago, we were accountable because if we didn't put food on the table, we starved. If we didn't chop firewood, we froze. The consequences of our actions were unavoidable and often severe. Today, through automation and advances in technology, we have made our environments almost ridiculously comfortable—achieving the highest level of comfort that human civilization has ever seen. We don't spend our days chasing food and seeking shelter. We have more than we need even if we can't afford it, because credit allows us to acquire things now and put off taking responsibility for them until some vague future date. As a result, we're able to insulate ourselves from consequences and from much of the reality of life. And that starts to erode our accountability bit by bit, because what holds us accountable is either ourselves or our environment. Once we've mastered the environment, the only thing left to hold us accountable … is us.

This goes against our DNA. Humans are programmed to exert the least amount of effort possible to accomplish what we need for basic survival—a trait that helped us stay alive in our hunter-gatherer days but doesn't really serve us now. Unfortunately, we keep our heads planted firmly in the sand, because it's easier (or we think it's easier). Until reality slaps us in the face and we literally can't be oblivious anymore. Like when Robert's college professor kicked him out.

Of course, Robert was hardly alone in his ignorance of what it took to get through college. A 2009 *New York Times* article on college students' increasing sense of entitlement cited a study by researchers at the University of California, Irvine, in which a third of students surveyed admitted to expecting B grades simply for showing up to class. That number shot up to a full 40 percent for those who also completed the required reading.[1] Things like demonstrating an understanding of the subject matter or turning in quality work were dismissed as nonessential, or essential only for those people who wanted to earn As. Basically, they expected the educational equivalent of a participation trophy—that you *deserve* something simply for showing up. And that creates a disconnect in their brain between what they were taught to expect and reality.

How does that work in real life? Well, imagine that the kid who shows up to class and does all their reading and thinks they're going to get a B gets a C or a D or even (heaven forbid) an F, because they can't demonstrate that they've actually learned anything. That grade is a consequence that might motivate them to change their behavior. But if they go to their professor and complain, and the professor feels sorry for them and says, "Okay, let's give you a B because you tried,"

---

1    Max Roosevelt, "Student Expectations Seen as Causing Grade Disputes," *New York Times*, February 17, 2009, https://www.nytimes.com/2009/02/18/education/18college.html.

then there's no motivation to actually learn the material. And when that student tries to get their master's degree, that's going to be harder. And if they get moved along, their PhD is going to be harder. Maybe they'll make it all the way through and enter the working world with an elite-level degree and no actual knowledge. But at some point, the consequences will catch up to them—and to whomever is unlucky enough to hire them.

We keep moving the goalposts of our expectations of life because it's hard to be the bad guy. It's hard to tell someone that their effort wasn't good enough and they have to face the consequences. But that's actually the smart thing—and the compassionate thing to do in the long run. Because the longer you delay facing a problem, the bigger it gets. If Johnny can't read in third grade but his teachers agree to let him move on to fourth grade, that's bad. If he still hasn't learned to read and they let him graduate from high school, that's a tragedy. But nobody ever wants to be the person who draws the line, including Johnny. Why would he, when he's getting by? It's so much easier to remain oblivious … until reality catches up with him and he's an eighteen-year-old high school graduate who is also functionally illiterate.

*The longer you delay facing a problem, the bigger it gets.*

How often does that actually happen? More often than you think. In 2014, a full 19 percent of high school graduates couldn't read, according to a US Department of Education study.[2] That same study also revealed that 14 percent of US adults, or around 32 million people, cannot read, and a full 21 percent of adults read below a fifth-grade level. And it all can be traced back to a lack of accountability.

2   National Assessment of Adult Literacy (NAAL), https://nces.ed.gov/naal/kf_demo-graphics.asp#3.

# The Price of Obliviousness

Since you're reading this book and therefore not included in those statistics, you may be asking, "What does it matter? What difference can something I'm not even aware of make in my life?" To be perfectly frank, it matters because, while you might not know it, you suffer. That's the price we all pay for lack of accountability. We don't always realize we're suffering, but we are. Maybe you feel vaguely unsatisfied with aspects of your life—or maybe you full-on hate your job, or know your marriage is terrible, or you're twenty-five pounds overweight and your doctor just told you you're prediabetic. But that just means you're unlucky, right? You're just one of those people who doesn't get what they want. Life seems to happen *to* you, while the things you want and dream about pass you by and happen for other people. At the same time, drama seems to follow you everywhere. Problems almost fall from the sky. And you have absolutely no idea why. You assume that all of this is completely beyond your control.

That's what being a victim means. You have no control.

Clearly, this state of unawareness is not a very comfortable place to be. But you wouldn't know it from the vast numbers of people who spend their lives there, oblivious to the simple things they can do that could help them have a better, more productive, happier life. But there is a simple solution to all this dissatisfaction. You just have to wake up. And we're going to help you do that right now.

# ACCOUNTABILITY EXERCISE: THE SATISFACTION WHEEL

When you're at the Lack of Awareness level of accountability, you're unaware that you're not satisfied. You've accepted that dissatisfaction as a part of your life, to the point that you don't even know it's there. The antidote to all this obliviousness is to face whatever it is you're not seeing. You have to look in the mirror.

The Satisfaction Wheel can be that mirror.

As you'll see on the next page, the Satisfaction Wheel is a simple exercise designed to help you move into awareness by taking a careful look at the areas where you're not satisfied in your life. The exercise actually has two wheels—one dedicated to your professional life and the other to your life outside of work. The center of the wheel represents complete dissatisfaction, and the outside edge equals 100 percent satisfaction. Your job is to assign each area in each wheel a number from one to ten indicating how satisfied you are in that area.

Keep in mind, this exercise was designed just to spark your awareness of those areas where you're not satisfied. It's not about solving the problem—yet. Since you can't solve a problem without first acknowledging the problem is there, this is a crucial first step. So go ahead and fill out your wheels.

# The Professional Satisfaction Wheel

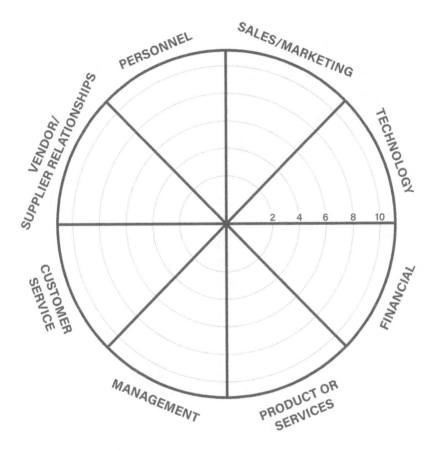

Download a full-size image of the satisfaction wheel for you to work on and keep separate from the book. Go to www.NobodyCaresBook.com or use this QR code to download the wheels.

# The Personal Satisfaction Wheel

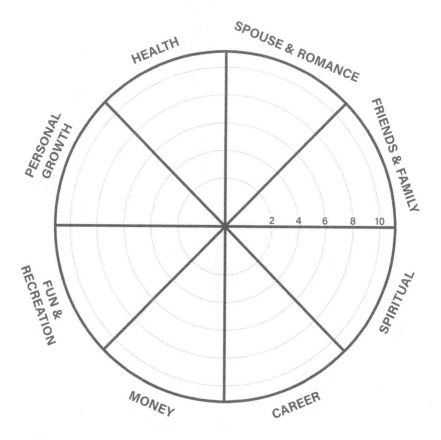

NOTE: Don't lie to yourself when doing this. Be honest—brutally honest. This (like all the exercises in this book) is just for you. No one else needs to know what you've written, so there's no reason to hide.

Take a good look at the levels of satisfaction reflected on your wheels. If you were unaware that you were dissatisfied a minute ago, now you know. You can look at your wheels and see exactly where you are not getting what you want out of life. That awareness is the first step to accountability. And it's also a challenge. You can't unsee what you have just seen. Once you become aware and recognize your responsibility in where you are today, you can never go back to obliviousness again.

So we're adding a second step to this first challenge to get you to flex your accountability muscle a little bit more and to use this new piece of knowledge you've gained about yourself.

Pick one of the areas on the wheel where your level of satisfaction is less than ten. Don't automatically try to tackle a two or even a three; we're just beginning to stretch your accountability muscle, so think of this as more of a warm-up than a full workout. Just pick one area where your life isn't a total horror show but could stand some improvement. Your challenge is to think about how you might change your behavior around that one thing you don't like.

That's it.

It may sound small, but one small change can be deceptively powerful. If one thing changes in the environment, it affects everything else. That's called the ripple effect , or a trophic cascade. One change leads to another, and another, and another, until the entire environment has shifted. It's how nature works, as demonstrated by the story of the reintroduction of wolves to Yellowstone National Park.

In the 1930s, the gray wolf was killed off in Yellowstone to protect the Yellowstone elk. With their biggest predator suddenly removed from the scene, the elk flourished, which was the point. The only problem was, they did that a little too well. The elk population expanded to the point that they decimated the vegetation and affected other animal populations by gobbling up their food supply. This was especially hard on the

*One small change can be deceptively powerful. If one thing changes in the environment, it affects everything else.*

beaver, which needed the willows the elk were eating to survive the winter. By 1995, there was only one beaver colony left in the park.

Luckily, that also happened to be the year the gray wolf was reintroduced to the Greater Yellowstone Ecosystem. And slowly but surely, the return of this missing element of the ecosystem turned things around. Today, the park is home to nine beaver colonies, just one aspect of the ripple effect caused by the wolves' return.[3]

The same kind of trophic cascade, or ripple effect, happens when you become accountable. It changes everything around you in large, small, and sometimes unexpected ways.

But we're getting ahead of ourselves. We promised to take this one step at a time, so in the next chapter, we'll tackle the next baby step up the Accountability Mountain—dealing with blame.

Oh, and by the way, in case you were wondering, when Robert came back to school the next semester, he signed up to take that class he was kicked out of and he got an A.

That's the power of accountability.

---

3    Brodie Farquhar, "Wolf Reintroduction Changes Ecosystem in Yellowstone," *Yellowstone National Park Trips*, June 30, 2021, https://www.yellowstonepark.com/things-to-do/wildlife/wolf-reintroduction-changes-ecosystem/.

Is this making sense?

Are you seeing how this can help you

live the life you really want?

Tell others about our book.

Take a photo of the book cover and share on

your favorite social media.

Let them know how this is affecting you and

send them to get a copy for themselves at

**www.NobodyCaresBook.com**

# CHAPTER TWO

## You Didn't Tell Me I'd Need Hiking Boots!

*The more we blame others, the worse we feel.*

—**LEO TOLSTOY**

Now is probably a good time to let you in on something we will remind you of a few times throughout the course of this book. We also struggle with accountability—all the time. We by no means are perfect in this area, but that's okay. Our goal is to inspire you to become victorious over the challenges in your life, just as we have learned to do.

When people first become aware of the need for accountability in their life, when they leave obliviousness behind and realize that there is, in fact, a problem, one of the first things they do is blame other people for that problem. It feels so natural that we do it without thinking about it—almost like a knee-jerk reaction to get us out of a situation. For example, take this incident that happened a few years ago with Robert and his then-sixteen-year-old son, James.

Robert had specifically set aside an hour or so to hang out and watch a TV show with James. He made a special appointment to spend time with his son, because family is important to him, and as a busy executive with a lot of commitments, he works to hold himself accountable for making sure that it happens. So on that day, Robert finished up whatever he had to do that day and was waiting for James to arrive ...

And he waited ... and waited ... and waited.

And after about an hour, Robert got a text from James:

*Hey, I'm running late.*

Uh … obviously. But that was it. No explanation. No apology. And no estimated time of arrival so his father could plan accordingly. Just *I'm running late.*

So Robert continued to wait. Another thirty minutes went by. Then another text came in. This one read as follows:

*Hey, I'll be there later. I'm on my way pretty soon.*

*Later? Pretty soon???* Again, no explanation, no apology, and no indication of when Robert might be able to stop waiting and start spending time with his son like they had planned.

It turned out he needed to wait another thirty minutes, because that's when, about an hour and a half after he was originally supposed to arrive, James finally graced the room with his presence.

His father looked to him for an explanation. And the first words out of James's mouth were …

No, not "I'm sorry."

Not "There was an emergency" either.

Nope. They were "Stupid Taco Bell."

Yes, according to James, *Taco Bell* was responsible for the fact that he was ninety minutes late to meet his dad.

You're probably pretty curious as to how that could possibly happen! Robert certainly was. So he asked his son, "What's that about?"

James launched into an explanation. "I waited forever for the order, and when they gave it to me, it was wrong, and I had to go back and get it fixed again because they messed up the order …"

All perfectly plausible. Except James had left out one crucial detail, which Robert couldn't help but notice.

"*Why* were you at Taco Bell?" he asked. "You were supposed to be here with me an hour and a half ago!"

"Well," James explained, "I went to my girlfriend's house and picked her up, and she wanted a taco, so I took her to Taco Bell to get a taco, and that's when …"

Well, that's when Robert cut him off.

"You shouldn't have picked up your girlfriend. You shouldn't have gone to Taco Bell. You should have come here like you were supposed to."

But that hadn't occurred to James. Because he was stuck at the next level of the Accountability Mountain: Blame.

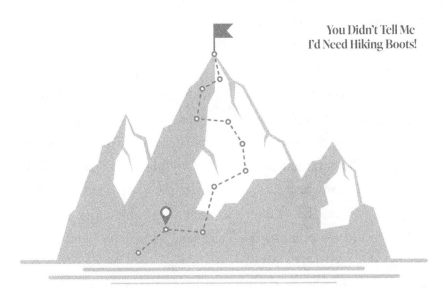

You Didn't Tell Me
I'd Need Hiking Boots!

## You Are Here

To call Blame another level of the Accountability Mountain isn't exactly fair, because it's down there in the mud and muck with lack of awareness, just maybe a tiny fraction of an inch above it. The only real difference is, when you're stuck at this level, you're at least aware that there's a problem, like James knew that he was late to meet his dad. But that's basically the full extent of your awareness. Instead of responding to what you know by moving to fix the problem or even address the problem, your brain immediately looks for the reason the problem is *not your fault*.

In other words, it's the opposite of owning it. It's pawning it off.

You know you're stuck at the Blame level of the Accountability Mountain when, while discussing something that went wrong or talking about why you're unhappy, another person's name comes out of your mouth. It doesn't even have to be a person. It can be an institution, like the government, or the "system," or a local fast food establishment.

In other words, it's not *you* that's making you unhappy or wrong. It's anything and everything but you.

And you're in good company, because absolutely everybody blames.

Think about it. Have you ever met a person who never blamed anything on anything or anyone? A person who has never, ever uttered anything along the lines of "my boss is a jerk" or "the traffic was terrible" or "I never got the email" or anything like that to explain their own actions or lack thereof? Even the Dalai Lama probably said, "You know, the weather out there is horrible today" at some point. We've been pointing the finger for as long as we humans have walked this earth—Eve blamed the snake, Adam blamed Eve, and what started back in the Garden of Eden is a not-so-proud tradition we've carried on to this day.

Because blaming is more than a habit; it's a *reflex*. It's actually hardwired in our brains. Meaning, yes, you can blame blame, at least in part, on biology.

# The Science of Blame

You may not like hearing it, but your brain is hardwired to treat you like a snowflake. All our brains are. We humans have this thing we do where, when things go well, we're quick to pat ourselves on the back and give ourselves credit for the outcome—but when things don't go so well, we attribute it to outside factors. Psychologists call this phenomenon *self-serving bias.*

It works like this. Say a project you're involved with at work gets a rave review from the higher-ups. It's human nature to congratulate yourself for a job well done and think about all the things *you did right* to contribute to that success. But if that same project crashes and burns? Chances are, in your mind, it will be because of something somebody else did. Maybe those idiot higher-ups can't see your genius. Or maybe that dumb idea they implemented instead of yours derailed the whole thing.

It's a similar phenomenon to *fundamental attribution error*, which *Simply Psychology* describes as "the tendency for people to overemphasize dispositional or personality-based explanations for behaviors observed in others while underemphasizing situational explanations."[4] In other words, when we see another person make a mistake or do something we don't approve of, we assume it happened because of what type of person they are as opposed to some outside force or circumstance. We judge them as responsible. But when *we* make a mistake, it's never our fault. It's the weather. Or our coworker. Or that darn Taco Bell.

All this finger pointing doesn't happen because we're bad people. It happens because the human brain wants to know "why," while the

---

4    Dr. Saul McLeod, "Fundamental Attribution Error," *Simply Psychology,* October 31, 2018, https://www.simplypsychology.org/fundamental-attribution.html.

human psyche prefers an answer that's not "me." It's also how the human response to the fear of consequence evolved. If we can just divert that consequence by diverting responsibility over to someone or something else, then we don't have to deal with the immediate pain—which is the actual thing we fear.

We learn how to do it when we're little kids. Imagine you're four years old, and every time you get caught stealing a cookie, your mom puts you in time out. You could stop stealing cookies, and maybe you even remember sitting in time out and thinking twice about stealing cookies a couple of times. But you're four, and chances are at some point you're going to slip up and grab a cookie when you shouldn't.

And when you do, and your mom asks, "Did you take that cookie?" you remember what's coming next. You're going to be sent to your room. Which you also know you do not want. So you point at your brother and say, "He did it!" And when Mom sends him to his room instead of you despite his protests, you learn that instead of having to face a consequence, you can successfully pass it on to some other entity.

Sorry, bro.

That's why Blame is so low on the Accountability Mountain. It's the easiest, fastest way to deal with the stress of having screwed up—pass it off to some other poor sucker, who may or may not wind up suffering the consequences on your behalf.

# The Blame Hall of Fame

The list of those poor suckers we blame is almost endless. Think of all the people we regularly deem responsible for the problems we face and the things that don't go our way. Mean teachers, bad bosses, evil exes, unmotivated employees, lazy or clueless coworkers, less-athletic teammates, parents who didn't love us enough or teach us what we needed to know, the system, the Man—the list goes on and on. It's not that there can't be a kernel of truth (or more than a kernel in some cases) to any one of these. There are bad bosses, unmotivated employees, and lazy and clueless coworkers out there (frequently at the same workplace!). There will be people whom you don't like, people who don't like you, people who don't share your values, people who don't recognize your talents, and people who do things that are just. Not. Fair. But as we've said before and will say again, so what? How much power can one person really have over your destiny?

(Answer: As much as you give them.)

This reminds us of another story about James (shout out to James, for allowing us to share his very normal adolescent mistakes with the world to prove our points!). He was struggling to do well in one of his classes, and Robert asked him why. James told him the reason his grades were so bad was because he had a really bad teacher who was a jerk.

Again, this was entirely possible. Some teachers are bad, some teachers are jerks, and some, unfortunately, are both. So Robert asked his son for some clarification.

*How much power can one person really have over your destiny? (Answer: As much as you give them.)*

"So," he asked, "is everybody having a hard time in that class?"

James just looked at him. So Robert went on.

"Because if the teacher's that bad, then everybody would be failing. Right?"

James had to admit that everybody in the class was not, in fact, failing.

So Robert asked, "If he's really so bad, how is it only affecting *you?*"

When something you describe as a problem for everyone only affects you, there's a more than reasonable chance *you're* the problem. That's a pretty obvious sign that you're stuck in Blame. But again, it's not like James was doing anything the rest of us haven't done. Our society likes to blame others. It's how we roll these days. We see it in our families, our work, and even our courts.

For example, back in 2002, two Bronx teenagers, Jazlyn Bradley and Ashley Pelman, sued the McDonald's Corporation and two local franchises for "making" them obese.[5] The girls were both huge McDonald's fans—Jazlyn actually ate there twice a day, stopping by for breakfast (a McMuffin) in the morning and coming back later in the day for a Big Mac meal and an apple pie. Ashley preferred the Happy Meals, especially the toys. And they were both, technically, obese. At nineteen, Jazlyn stood five feet, six inches tall and weighed 270 pounds, and while fourteen-year-old Ashley weighed 100 pounds less at 170, she was only four feet, ten inches tall.

> *When something you describe as a problem for everyone only affects you, there's a more than reasonable chance you're the problem.*

So they sued. Or, more specifically, they retained a lawyer who filed a lawsuit claiming that McDonald's and two Bronx franchises owed the teens damages because they failed to provide information about the health risks associated with its food.

Mercifully, the judge did not agree, and the case was dismissed in 2003. However, in case you think this is some kind of once-in-

---

5    Marc Santora, "Teenagers' Suit Says McDonald's Made Them Obese," *New York Times,* November 21, 2002, https://www.nytimes.com/2002/11/21/nyregion/teenagers-suit-says-mcdonald-s-made-them-obese.html.

a-lifetime thing, Jazlyn and Ashley weren't the only people to take Mickey D's to court for making them fat. Not that year. Not even in their neighborhood that year. Because, also in 2001, a Bronx man named Caesar Barber filed a class action lawsuit against McDonald's, Burger King, Wendy's, and KFC, accusing all four of the fast-food titans of making him and his fellow New Yorkers sick with their salty and fatty (yet oh-so-tasty) food offerings.[6]

And James thought Taco Bell was the problem ...

That suit was also dismissed—a win for accountability! However, regardless of how well Blame holds up under the law, the tendency to look for someone or something to hold responsible for our own actions persists and pervades every aspect of our lives. Even though all this finger pointing and buck passing doesn't do anything for any of us.

In fact, it's more like a prison.

## The High Cost of Blame

What's so bad about blame, especially if everyone does it? Honestly, what's bad is that it hurts *you*. When you blame other people or things, it may divert consequences in the short term, but ultimately you're the one who pays the price. You make whatever problem was there in the first place worse, because when you don't take responsibility for anything, you can't actually get any better at anything. In fact, you're propagating the chance that you're going to screw up again, because you're not owning it enough to motivate yourself to want to get better. What works in the moment will, in the long term, rob you of an opportunity to improve. And that keeps you a victim.

---

6   Geraldine Sealey, "Obese Man Sues Fast-Food Chains," *ABC News*, January 7, 2006, https://abcnews.go.com/amp/US/story?id=91427&page=1.

When you blame, you feel powerless to change anything, because if you're not responsible, what can you do? Bottom line, you're making it worse for yourself because you never improve to the point where you can avoid the thing that makes you unhappy or gets you in trouble in the first place. You may be postponing pain, but it's going to come back and bite you on the you-know-what at some point down the line. When you never move to a place of accountability, you're constantly deferring consequences. And when you defer consequences, you're ultimately deferring a better life. You're pushing that day when you're finally happy and your life finally looks something like the life you want further and further into the future.

Besides if you're "not the problem" or you don't accept your role in the problem, you can't be the solution. If the problem is that guy over there, or the weather, or the kid who filled your order at Taco Bell, there's not a whole lot you can do about it. Once again, you're a victim. But if you own it, if you acknowledge how and where you are the problem, you can fix it, and eventually you can be victorious. Regardless of the circumstances.

For example, say you work for a company that's going through a rough period. If you own that company and you're not meeting your sales goals or you're losing out to the competition or whatever, the answer is pretty simple. You need to take responsibility and fix your company. It doesn't matter if your employees are clueless or lazy or unmotivated, or if the competition cuts corners, or if your marketing agency sucks. You're the owner, so by definition you own it.

But what if you don't own the company? What if you just work there, it's your jerk boss making all those bad decisions that are dragging you and everybody else down, and it has nothing to do with you? Well, in that case, you have a few choices:

1.  You can stay there and continue to blame your boss for how much everything sucks and be a victim.

2.  You can own it by taking responsibility for any part you might have played in making things a hot mess and doing what you can to fix it. By doing that, you will help yourself and maybe help the company, and you will be victorious.

3.  You can also own it by making a choice to move to a less toxic work environment and take concrete steps to find another, better job. Then you can be victorious someplace else.

The point is, you're not powerless. You don't have to be a victim. But you will be as long as you blame, because when you do, you give the power over your situation to the person or thing you're blaming. That means that person or thing controls you. Whereas when you own it and say, "I screwed up. I did this, and it was wrong and therefore I'm going to fix what I did. I'm going to own my part and focus on that," you're the one in control. And that means you're free. Maybe you don't feel all that free right now. But stick with us, and we will help you get there.

# Okay, But What About Extenuating Circumstances?

Of course, there are people and entities out there in the world that are deserving of at least a little blame. McDonald's didn't exactly design their menu with public health in mind, and their commercials don't include warnings that eating their food every day could possibly be a health hazard. And, as we acknowledged before, we're all the product of different circumstances, and our backgrounds, what we've learned, what tools we've had access to, who raised us, and a million other things all play a part in where we end up. But there's a point at which we have to look around at where we have ended up—where we are—and ask, "What now?"

Recently, we were lucky enough to meet a man named Nicholas James Vujicic, who, while living a very successful life, also happens to have no arms and no legs. Obviously, it would be easy for this guy to blame God and the world and be bitter and sullen and hopeless. You think life is unfair? Ask a guy with no arms or legs how fair life is! But Nicholas made a choice that he was not going to be that way. He decided to live his life to its fullest to the best of his ability. He found a woman who loved him, and they got married, and today they have *four* kids. But more importantly, he's living the life he wants to live. He's in control of his destiny. And he's definitely not a victim. Why? Because, at the end of the day, he looked at himself and his reality and said, "I have no arms or legs. What now?"

Those two words, *what now,* are the key to pulling yourself out of the muck and up past this level of the Accountability Mountain.

## So What About What Now?

By now we've established that while blaming someone or something may make you feel better (for a while), it does not fix the problem—because you often *are* the problem. Of course, this is your life, and since it's your life, you can blame whatever or whomever you want, for whatever you want, whenever you want. You have that freedom. But here's the thing. No matter what it gets you out of in the short term, blame will eventually rob you of your freedom, because it's a prison—and nobody else even knows it's there. Nobody else knows about all this blame that you're holding on to except you, and how it's holding you back and keeping you unhappy and dissatisfied. They're all just going along with their lives, worrying about their own problems, dealing with their own baggage. So you can be as miserable as you want to be. No one really cares.

Or, you can consciously fight that impulse and rise above blaming. In order to do that, you need to

- be aware of blame,

- look at the places where you have blame, and

- have a process or some tools in place for stopping blame.

We're going to help you do all three of these things right now.

# The What-Now Tool

One tool that works really well is this: when you start to blame somebody, ask yourself, "So then what? What now? What am I going to do about it?" For example, imagine you aren't making enough money at your job to afford to live where you want to live. Instead of blaming your boss who doesn't appreciate you or your cheapskate company or the fact that you only went to a mediocre state school, stop and ask yourself, "What now? What am I going to do about it?" Because while blaming any or all of those things might make you feel better in the moment, it isn't going to do anything to fix the problem: you're dissatisfied with where you live. Whereas boosting your skills or improving your relationships in order to make more money, or researching neighborhoods you like that you can afford, or doing any number of other things to fix the actual problem will make you feel a lot better for a lot longer.

# ACCOUNTABILITY EXERCISE: TRACKING BLAME

This exercise is going to bring us back to the Accountability Wheel you filled out in the last chapter. This time, we're going to dig a little deeper and use the wheel to figure out where blame is having an impact on your life.

Look back at your two wheels and focus on one of the areas of dissatisfaction. Again, you want to look for those places where you're not a ten, and maybe even not quite a five. Focus on just one of those areas and ask yourself, "Why am I dissatisfied with this aspect of my life?"

If the first answer that pops into your head is another person or thing, congratulations! You've uncovered a place where you're blaming. Which means you can start to deal with it:

1. Zero in on that person or thing you named as the reason for your dissatisfaction.

2. Now answer these two questions, and write down those answers.

   a. What responsibility does the person or thing I'm blaming actually have for this issue in my life?

   b. What responsibilities do I have regarding that same issue?

3. Run through this exercise with each of the areas where you are less than satisfied.

The next time you feel the urge to blame someone or something for your dissatisfaction, refer back to these lists. It will get you out of victim mode by showing you what you can actually do and control to improve your situation.

Now that you know how to tackle blame, we'll move up (but only slightly) the mountain to the next accountability killer: excuses.

# CHAPTER THREE

## My Gear Is Heavy!

*He that is good for excuses is seldom good for anything else.*

## —BENJAMIN FRANKLIN

Robert's business was not doing well. Not that he wasn't good at what he did, bringing businesspeople from across a variety of different fields and walks of life together and facilitating conversations that helped them grow professionally and personally. Robert loved to do that more than almost anything, and he could do it with his eyes closed and both hands tied behind his back. That was in his wheelhouse. It was why he got up in the morning, or at least part of why.

But now, it was all at risk.

The problem was, Robert couldn't get enough CEOs and business owners to sign up for his peer groups. No matter how good he was at what he did, or how much he loved it, or how much his clients grew from it, or how much he dedicated his life to it, it struggled to become a successful business. If things didn't change, he wouldn't be able to do it anymore.

And Robert knew the terrible, horrible, awful truth about why he was in this sad state of affairs.

*He couldn't sell.*

This was, in Robert's mind, an indisputable fact. Maybe you feel that way about sales too—a lot of people do. It's a very common belief that some people are just natural born salespeople and others of us are not, and Robert, sadly, knew he was one of the unfortunate souls in the latter category. But, hey, he was comfortable with that. After all, nobody's good at everything, and a lot of people aren't good at sales.

Besides, it wasn't like he didn't *want* to be better at it. Of course he would have liked to improve, to learn what it took to be better, but he had a business to run—all by himself, for heaven's sake! Where was he going to find the time? If things in the business were better, he could hire someone to help him with sales, but if he could afford to hire someone to help him with sales, *that would mean he didn't need help with sales!* Bottom line, Robert felt stuck. His business was not going to grow, it was possibly even going to fail, and there was nothing he could do about it because he was terrible at sales and therefore it was *not his fault!*

Of course, by now you've probably figured out that the problem wasn't really that Robert was terrible at sales. The problem was that he was trapped on the next level of the Accountability Mountain: Excuses.

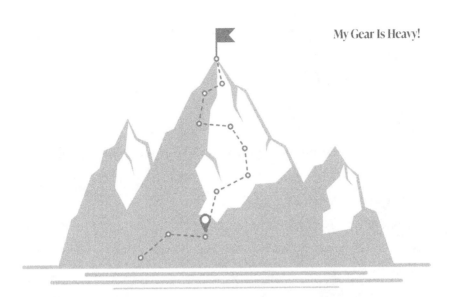

# You Are Here

When the first words out of your mouth are some version of "It's not my fault because …," you're most likely trapped at the Excuses level of the Accountability Mountain. The good news is, you've risen above the worst of the muck and mud, because you're no longer flinging the blame for your problems at some other poor sucker or institution or inanimate object. So you're *sort of* owning it …

Except, in reality, you're absolutely not.

In reality, Excuses and Blame are almost like evil twins. Yes, you have some awareness that there's a problem. However, your immediate reaction to that awareness is to defer responsibility for the problem. The difference that elevates Excuses about a fraction of an inch above Blame is that there's some truth in it. You recognize there's something about you that could be contributing to whatever problem you're having. But sitting right alongside that truth is one massive lie:

*You can't do anything about it.*

That one tiny lie conveniently absolves you of all responsibility. Say someone asked your grandmother, who uses a wheelchair, to run a four-minute mile? Of course she can't do that, and it's definitely not her fault! Therefore, it's wrong to expect her to. Well, using that logic, it was also wrong for anyone, including Robert, to expect him to be able to sell. After all, as Robert would have put it, being bad at sales was "just the way I am."

You hear that phrase a lot when you're at the Excuses level of the Accountability Mountain: "I'm terrible at math—that's just the way I am. I can't lose weight—that's just the way I am." You're basically saying that you're not smart enough or strong enough or—let's just say it—*good enough* to be accountable. At least, that's what you tell yourself when you're trapped in Excuses. They're all about telling yourself and the world why it's okay for you to be insufficient, or unhappy in your life, or not doing the things you want. Why you *can't* be victorious. Because it's *not your fault* you're unhappy or wrong. You've just reached the limits of your capabilities. You can't possibly do any more. You have no choice except to be a victim.

## Why Do We Make Excuses?

If excuses make us victims, why do we retreat to this position of victimhood over and over again? The first and most obvious reason is that excuses provide a quick exit from accountability. You're saying, "Hey, I recognize this is a problem, but there's nothing I can do about it." And then you're done. You don't have to worry about it anymore. You've removed yourself from the conversation.

Of course, we all have things we're good at and other things that we're not so good at—like Robert and sales. We tend to forget that the way to get better at those things we're not good at is by working at them. You know, practice. That's how we all learned to walk and talk and read and write. We tried and failed and tried again until we figured it out. Some things came easier than others, but that didn't mean we stopped trying.

Until we got older and realized that maybe this accountability stuff was a little too scary. That's natural. As you move up the Accountability Mountain, you're going to look for reasons to turn around. You panic. Because "up" can be a very frightening place to go. You're entering unfamiliar territory where you don't know what will happen. There are fewer people around you. You feel exposed.

But that's not even the only reason we've grown so comfortable with excuses. Another is our definition of success. We tend to hold up impossible images of what "doing something" means. Being "good at math" doesn't mean passing your classes and being able to figure out the tip on a restaurant bill without a calculator. It means you're doing quantum equations like Stephen Hawking. Being a successful businessperson doesn't mean serving enough clients to be able to support yourself and your family and realize some of your dreams. It means running a billion-dollar corporation and going to space like Richard Branson or Jeff Bezos.

You can't possibly achieve those things because there's no way you could ever imagine doing it. You're not Stephen Hawking or Richard Branson! So why even try?

For starters, because equating math skills with Stephen Hawking or business success with Jeff Bezos isn't the *truth*. There are countless successful businesspeople who will never, ever earn a billion dollars. You can be an ace at math and still not be capable of unraveling the mysteries of the universe. But that's not what we sell when we talk about success. In our society, we sell the pinnacle as the goal. As opposed to the very good and valid and real things 99 percent of us will achieve through a minor amount of work. But equating success with the highest of the high provides an easy out. It's a standard you'll never live up to. It's the ultimate "I can't. So why even try?"

On top of that (because there are almost as many reasons for excuses as there are excuses), our society is also obsessed with instant gratification. We want to be good at things without having to go through the work required to do them. Well, it takes work to accomplish anything, but actual *mastery* requires more than just work. It requires sacrifice. And at the very least, getting past where you are requires you to do something more than you're currently doing.

However, as we mentioned previously, human beings are programmed to put out the least amount of effort possible. So instead of doing those things we're not "good at," we make an excuse. It's much more convenient to say, "Oh, I'm just too dumb to learn this," or "I'm just not an athlete" than to try and possibly fail. It's so much easier (and less risky) to accept that excuse and be done with it.

## Our Bodies, Our Excuses

To understand the power of excuses, you only need to look at an area where they're so dangerous they're actually killing people. That area would be health and fitness. At this point, you'd have to be living under a rock not to know that being overweight and/or unfit is hazardous to your health. Yet according to the Centers for Disease Control and Prevention (CDC), over 42 percent of Americans aged twenty and over were obese in 2017–2018, a rise of almost 12 percent in less than two decades.[7] And at the same time, specifically in 2018, the CDC also reported that less than 23 percent of adults aged eighteen to sixty-four got the recommended amount of both aerobic

---

7    "Adult Obesity Facts," Centers for Disease Control and Prevention, accessed April 5, 2022, https://www.cdc.gov/obesity/data/adult.html.

and muscle-strengthening exercise.[8] And in 2018, just under half of all Americans met the CDC guidelines for getting enough physical activity to improve their health.[9]

That adds up to a lot of people making a lot of excuses.

Even among those people who do exercise, excuses are still an issue. Salem used to work as a personal trainer, so has heard at least a million of these types of excuses. He loved (and still loves) physical fitness and wanted to pass that passion on to other people. And he did. But along the way, he also heard enough excuses to fill this book and a couple more.

Personal training is hard work. It's sweaty, and it takes effort—effort Salem's clients signed up for and were paying for! They must have expected to work hard on some level, since they were paying a professional to make them work hard. Yet when it came to actually doing that hard work, those same paying clients hit him with a myriad of personal excuses.

For example, Salem had one male client that he asked to do some squats. The client immediately came back with an excuse. "Well, I got a bad back, so I can't do squats and I can't do dead lifts." This could have been a real issue, so Salem tried to get the guy to explain his back problems in more detail so he could make an adjustment or find a work-around so the guy could still get the workout he paid for. But when he asked his client, "What's so bad about your back?" he didn't get a specific answer.

So he asked a more specific question. "Do you mean you can't right now, just with your body weight, squat down?"

---

8     Sarah Gray, "A Shocking Percentage of Americans Don't Exercise Enough, CDC Says," *Fortune*, June 28, 2018, https://fortune.com/2018/06/28/americans-do-not-exercise-enough-cdc/amp/.

9     "More People Walk to Better Health," Centers for Disease Control and Prevention, August, 2012, https://www.cdc.gov/vitalsigns/walking/index.html.

"No," the client said. "I can do that."

Meaning the client could do *something*, but he instead chose to focus on what he couldn't do in order to limit Salem's expectations of his performance.

That's another reason we make excuses, by the way. To limit other people's expectations of what we can do.

Salem worked with this client, step by step, to challenge his excuses and move him past his blocks. He started with body weight exercises. He asked, "How's your back feel?"

"Fine," said the client.

So Salem added a little weight. "Let's do something with a twenty-pound weight. How's your back now?"

"It feels good."

And—surprise! Within a few months, the client was doing squats and dead lifts and everything he'd sworn up and down that he couldn't do. And he was completely floored by this! How could he do all these things with his bad back?

Because, as Salem pointed out, the problem was never his back. The problem was his excuses, which created a self-fulfilling prophecy, because by *not* doing the types of exercises he was avoiding, he failed to strengthen his back, which made it worse.

Of course, this is no surprise to anyone who has worked in or with health and fitness. People tell themselves they can't do something because it's inconvenient or it's hard to do and doom themselves to a life of horrible health. Think about all the excuses that apply just to this area:

"I'm not an athlete."

"I don't have time."

"I'm big boned."

"I'm not coordinated."

"It's genetic."

"I'm too busy."

And on and on and on. And eventually, most of us just accept these excuses as reality without actually questioning what the consequences are and if we are okay with those consequences. Until one day your doctor says, "So you're going to have diabetes. Are you okay with that?"

"Well, no, I'm not okay with that. I don't want diabetes."

So if you don't want diabetes, what are you going to do to stop it?

Because, honestly, doing something to stop it is *not that hard*.

The Cooper Clinic in Dallas did a study and discovered that a person's quality of life will dramatically increase if they just walk thirty minutes four times a week. That's it. This is the same clinic that developed aerobics and was a big booster of rigorous exercise back in the 1970s and 1980s—but they're not advocating anything the average person can't do. Harvard Medical School recently published a study that says walking just two and a half hours a week, or twenty-two minutes a day, could reduce heart disease risk by 30 percent.[10]

So why don't more average people do it?

Because they don't want to leave the most dangerous zone of all—the comfort zone.

## Trapped in the Comfort Zone

People like to use the term *comfort zone* as an excuse for why they don't do something. "Oh, I could never ask my boss for a raise—it's outside my comfort zone. I can't do push-ups—they're outside my comfort zone." But *comfort zone* is really just another term for fear. When someone says,

---

10    "Walking for Health," *Harvard Health Publishing,* https://www.health.harvard.edu/exercise-and-fitness/walking-for-health.

"Well, I couldn't go talk to that person—it's outside my comfort zone," it's a lot more socially acceptable than "I can't go talk to that person—I'm scared." Most of us are uncomfortable admitting when we're afraid. So we use a really comfortable term that everyone understands—"that's out of my comfort zone"—and somehow that makes us feel better.

But it's really not about comfort zones at all. It's about the effort, right? This effort is not convenient. It doesn't always pay off. There's not a guarantee. But in society today, we don't have to do a lot of the work. We have removed it. Video game culture really helps with this. You don't like the outcome or whatever else, you just press reset and go do it again. Or you buy cheat codes. There are so many ways to get to that point where you don't have to put in the hard work it takes to be an expert, or to get what you want out of life, that we almost never have to try. And since that's an area where there's really no one else to blame, we explain that "that's just the way I am."

And "that's just the way I am" is a lie.

It's very easy to lie to ourselves. "Oh, I just procrastinate. I'm a procrastinator." But if you decide to accept that about yourself, you're basically saying, "I can't get my work done on time. It's simply not possible for me." And that's not actually true. You may struggle to finish your work on time. It may be hard for your brain. But that doesn't mean it's reality. The reality is that it will take you more work, not that it can't be done.

Robert grew up poor, with an abusive father, and had some challenging times in his life when he was a kid. But whenever he would say, "I can't," his mother would always come back with, "If you argue for your limits, they become your limits. So instead of spending all your time telling me what you can't do, what *can* you do?"

If you argue and argue about why you can't do something, eventually you'll be right. You won't be able to do it because you've talked yourself out of it. It's that self-fulfilling prophecy again. So what can you do to stop this vicious cycle?

## Getting Past Your Excuses

The dirty little secret about most of us is, we're afraid to be successful. It is our greatest fear, because success will take us away from everything that's familiar. It will, out of necessity, force us out of our precious comfort zones. And we don't want that. So we provide ourselves with excuses and tell ourselves what our limitations are, and that allows us to sit in the dark.

Deep down inside, most of us don't really believe in ourselves. There's so much head trash bouncing around in there that we

> *If you argue and argue about why you can't do something, eventually you'll be right. You won't be able to do it because you've talked yourself out of it.*

self-sabotage. But there's a good reason we're so insecure, and that is that we know ourselves pretty well. We know our dirty little secrets. We know how stupid, irresponsible, lazy, evil, selfish, untalented, unspecial, and just all-around lame we are. Contrary to what we post on our Facebook or Instagram pages, we know the real us, and we know it ain't pretty.

But do we really?

When you look at someone who's really successful or athletic or happy or whatever you're not and say, "There's no way I can do that. I'm not that guy," it's not because you're this super self-aware, brutally honest person who's just telling it like it is. It's because you're focused on the bad parts of yourself—and you're putting your focus there for a reason. Because it gives you an excuse to stop. It's a way to turn back and stay down in the muck of your comfort zone, where it's warm and safe, even if it's not quite as comfortable as you think it is.

We want you to stop doing that. We want you to stop looking at the bad parts of you, the things you can't do, the things you don't feel good about, and look for the good that's in there. Because there's an awful lot of hope and grace and kindness and mercy that's still there, buried under all the blame and excuses and obliviousness.

You've just got to look for it—or even just look at it.

Not that it's going to be easy to give up your personal excuses and start moving forward. It takes courage. But that courage can pay off. When you stand up and you say, "I'm not an athlete, but I'm still going to make the soccer team. I may not be the best player on the soccer team, but I'm going to play," you're defining what you really want—to play soccer on that soccer team. Not to be the best athlete. Although, if you wanted to be the best athlete, you could try harder and get some training and see if it happened. It might be harder for you than for the person who was born super athletic. But maybe you have a better advantage *because* of all that hard work it takes to get you there. It's a different journey, and it's your journey, and it will take you to a different place.

The positive side of all of this is that the thing you're avoiding, the thing you're afraid of, the thing that's holding you back is not nearly as tough as you think it is. Most of the time, the small amount of work it takes to simply not accept your personal excuse and not stop at "this is just who I am" will get you a long way. Just think about that twenty-two minutes of walking a day.

# Tools to Help

Sometimes, all you need to get past your personal excuses is a little reality check. How bad do you really have it? Say you're a woman in business and you feel you've hit a glass ceiling. You've worked at the same company for sixteen years and been passed over for promotions thirteen times. Yeah, that certainly stinks. But compare it to what it would be like to live in a country where women aren't allowed to get an education, let alone work, and their husbands can publicly beat them or chain them. You may be in a bad work situation, but you're not a prisoner. You

*The thing you're avoiding, the thing you're afraid of, the thing that's holding you back is not nearly as tough as you think it is.*

have options—you just can't always see them. Especially when you look at the whole problem instead of focusing on the first step.

That's why it helps to have a vision. You want something to propel you past your personal excuses that tell you you're not worthy, you can't do it, the world is against you, or *insert-your-excuse here*. One great way to kick-start this process is to talk to people who have already done what you're trying to do. If you wanted to climb Mount Everest, you wouldn't just head over to Nepal, strap on some boots, and start climbing. You'd talk to someone who has already done it, to get a better understanding of the journey ahead.

The same strategy applies to anything you want to try. At this first stage of the journey, of course there's a lot of fear of moving forward. You don't know what's going to happen! So it only makes sense that what removes that fear is *knowledge*. Once you start bringing in some knowledge around your situation, your brain can begin to understand, envision, and put a vision together of what your journey is going to look like and what to expect. And that makes it a lot less scary.

Robert always tells his clients that the difference between stress and pressure is knowledge. Stress comes from not knowing what you're doing. "How the hell am I going to get through this? Oh my gosh, the world's falling apart. What am I going to do?" But when you add knowledge to the equation, everything calms down. You can talk to someone about what they know. You can do research. You can put some milestones on the calendar and figure out how to reach them. And all of a sudden, you have a plan for moving forward instead of spinning around in circles, because you brought knowledge into the equation. Once you do that, and create a plan to get where you're going, you have the pressure to go get it done.

So the next time you find yourself saying "I can't," go get the knowledge you need to move from a hopeless situation to a plan. Then you can pressure yourself to make it happen.

## Turning Buts into Ands

One clue to the fact that you're making an excuse is the presence of the word "but." When you say things like …

"I need a new car, but I don't have a job."

"I deserved that promotion, but my coworker hogs all the attention and never gives me credit."

"I'd like to have a better relationship with my sister, but she's messed up …"

… that means you're living life as a victim. In fact, the power of that one little word is pretty amazing. That single three-letter word is probably the most vicious word in our vocabulary—because it instantly shuts the possibility of accountability down.

So here's a trick to dealing with the *buts* in your life. The next time you hear yourself use *but* in a sentence, stop, replace it with *and*, and then try to complete your sentence. If the sentence still works, fine. But if it doesn't, it usually means you need to add an action at the end of it.

For example, let's go back to that first example: "I need a new car, but I don't have a job." If you change it to "I need a new car, *and* I don't have a job," it may make sense grammatically, but otherwise there's obviously a missing thought there. So you need to finish the sentence. And right there, where you finish the sentence, is where you move to a place of accountability. So you say, "I need a new car, and I don't have a job, so I think I'll go get a job part time with my cousin's construction company, and then I'll make enough money to get a new car." Where the *but* stopped you, the *and* moves you forward to a place of action.

## ACCOUNTABILITY EXERCISE: I CAN'T BECAUSE I'M NOT ...

We all have things we think we're not capable of doing. But are we right about our limitations, or are there things we're not seeing? This exercise will help you separate the things you really can't do from the personal excuses that prevent you from doing everything you can.

1. Start by making a list of all those things you can't do. Maybe you can't shoot a basketball, or speak a foreign language, or ride a skateboard, or parallel park. Or maybe you can't do any of them. And maybe you don't care! Look for the things that you know you can't do that matter to you, and write those things down.

2. Now, go through your list and write down *why* you can't do each of those things. In other words, go ahead and make that excuse.

3. Now, look at the excuse you made, and ask yourself, "Is this reality or not? Could I do something to change the situation?" Is there a way you could gain the knowledge you need to be able to do the thing you think you can't do, like practicing shooting a basketball, or taking a driving lesson? Write that down next.

4. The moment you do that, that excuse is eliminated.

This same process can be used to gain a deeper understanding of your answers on the Satisfaction Wheels. So that's where we're going to go now.

1. Once again, we want you to start by focusing on an area where your satisfaction score is low.

2. Ask yourself, "Why am I at (whatever the number is)?" List all the reasons (or excuses) that explain why you are at that number.

3. Look at your lists of "reasons." Are they truths? Are they realities? If a reason is, in fact, true, go ahead and write "truth" next to it. If it's not true, if it's not "just the way you are" and you have the power to change it, write "lie."

4. Do this with all the areas of dissatisfaction on your wheels.

5. Now go back to your wheels and imagine what it would be like if an area where your score is low had a higher score. What would it take to get your satisfaction to six? What would it look like if it was all the way up at eight?

6. Hold on to that vision—because it can become the engine that will drive you past your personal excuses.

Hold on to those truths and the knowledge you've gained as we grow your accountability and climb higher up the mountain. You've already acknowledged that there are things in your life that you're not satisfied with, that you've blamed others for those things, and now, that you've used excuses to avoid accountability for them. Now, we're going to take on the rest of those lies and smash them to bits—beginning with the next one … that it's too hard.

# CHAPTER FOUR

## I'll Never Get Up This Slope

*Whether you think you can,*
*or you think you can't—you're right.*

—**HENRY FORD**

When Salem was a freshman in high school, he joined the swim team. He was a great swimmer, and, while he'd never done any competitive swimming before, he figured he'd easily pick up the tricks and strategies he needed to be able to compete. He started going to practice and wound up excelling in the backstroke and the breaststroke. It was all good ...

Until one day, at a swim meet, his coach decided to enter him in the two-hundred-meter individual medley, known to swimmers as the 200 IM.

In case you're not familiar with the ins and outs of competitive swimming, the individual medley is extra challenging because it includes all four competitive strokes: butterfly, backstroke, breaststroke, and freestyle. No swimmer is equally strong in all four, but for Salem, competing in the IM meant he would have to swim fifty competitive meters of a stroke he hadn't really mastered yet—the butterfly.

You know that famous image of the Olympic swimmer Michael Phelps rising up out of the water, his arms out to the sides? That's the butterfly. It's notorious for being the hardest stroke for a newbie swimmer to master, because you have to coordinate swinging your arms around your body simultaneously and pulling yourself through the water, which is weird enough on its own, while kicking with your legs held together like a dolphin. Once you get it and figure out how to put the pieces together, it's the fastest stroke, but until you do, the whole thing feels unnatural, clunky, and awkward.

It also happens to be the first stroke in the individual medley.

So, when the time came for the 200 IM, Salem was understandably nervous. He was a freshman, the smallest kid on the team, and about to swim the butterfly in competition for the very first time. As he stepped up on the diving block, looking right and left down the line of swimmers, he couldn't help thinking there was no way he was coming in any place but last. Honestly, he didn't even want to be there. His coach entered him in the event to "develop" him, which, at least to Salem, suddenly seemed like a very bad idea.

As he waited for the race to start, his mind continued to spin. *Why am I up here? I can't do this. There's no way I can do this.* The swimmers were given the signal to get ready, so Salem crouched down into the diving position with the rest of the competitors. Then the buzzer went off, signaling the start of the race, and everyone dived into the water and took off for the other end of the pool.

Everyone except Salem.

Salem got up from his crouching position, but instead of diving into the pool with the other swimmers, he just kind of stood there, watching them moving farther and farther away. He could hear his coaches and some of the spectators yelling, "Go! GO!" But he couldn't move. He was frozen in that spot, standing there on the diving block, as if his entire body was saying, "Don't do it."

When you think about it, it made absolutely no sense. It's not like Salem didn't know how to swim. He even knew how to swim the butterfly, just not very well. Meaning he was not going to drown, or even get hurt. But he just kept standing there, considering all of the possibilities, and imagining all of those possibilities as negative.

After about fifteen seconds, the words *jump in*, probably yelled by his coach, finally registered in his mind, and he jumped. But those fifteen seconds felt like an eternity.

An eternity stuck at the It's Too Hard level of the Accountability Mountain.

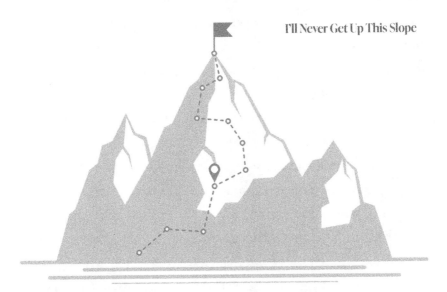

I'll Never Get Up This Slope

## You Are Here

When you feel like you've done all you can to achieve your goal and can go no further, you're probably at the It's Too Hard level of accountability. And before *we* go any further, we want to acknowledge that just getting here is an accomplishment. You've finally climbed out of the muck of obliviousness, blaming others, and making excuses.

That's more than some people ever do. You're aware that there is a problem, and you know there's no way to pass that problem off to another person or thing.

But you're also pretty darn sure that you can't do anything about it.

You've been climbing up the mountain, making your way out of the muck, moving along the trail, making progress, and it's like all of a sudden you come around a corner and there's a massive boulder blocking your path. You can't see any way around the boulder, or over it, or any way to get past it. So you stop.

What can you do? It's not that you don't *want* to own it. You would if you could. You just can't get past that boulder. It's impossible.

And, since you think you've gone as far as you think you can go and reached the limit of what you believe you can do (after all, passing that boulder is *impossible*), you believe you're being accountable.

But you're not.

You've reached the Valley of False Accountability, which encompasses the next two levels of our journey.

What both of these levels have in common is that when you're making your way through this valley, you think you're owning it, but you're really not. Because when you tell yourself that you've done everything you can, that there's no way you can climb over or around that boulder, that it's *too hard,* that's a justification for staying where you are. You can't get past the obstacle, so you can't actually own it. And that means you're still a victim.

You know you're at the It's Too Hard level of accountability when you hear yourself saying things like "I'm not ready," "I don't know how," or, obviously, "It's too hard." Same with "I could never ..." and "There's no way." Not that saying any of this is the most terrible, unforgivable sin in the world. We all do it. We all say "I can't" about something, or even several things. Maybe you say it about things you'd never, ever try, like bodybuilding or advanced trigonometry or going vegan. Maybe you say it about things you've tried once or twice but found too difficult to master or stick to, like quitting smoking. So yes, saying "It's too hard" is normal. But it's also keeping you a victim.

# Why We Do It

When you think about it, telling yourself you can't do something without even trying, or at least before giving it a decent amount of effort, is completely illogical. In fact, it's a lie. How can you know you can't do something until you try? That actually *is* impossible. Yet we tell ourselves we can't all the time. Why do we keep doing something that only holds us back?

One big reason is, everyone can relate to something being "too hard." We get plenty of support from the people around us, for the simple reason that they all feel the same way about something. Everyone has a moment when they think they're not capable, or that it's too scary, or they're too worried about making the wrong choice to move forward. For example, imagine you're unemployed, and somebody offers you a job for $40,000 a year less than you were making at your last job. Your first reaction will probably be "I can't afford to take that job. I won't be able to pay my bills. I have to keep looking." And if you tell your friends, "I was offered a job, but for $40K less than my last job, I couldn't take it," they'll all probably agree that the salary was too low and that you, in fact, could not take it. That's something the world would find perfectly acceptable.

But it's also a lie. Because you *can* take the job. There's nothing physically preventing you from taking the job. You've even been offered the job—meaning you could be making more money than you're making now, which we assume is zero dollars, within days.

The truth is, you don't *want* to take the job.

So the real question is ... *Why not?*

Generally, we find ourselves saying "It's too hard" when our problems get a little bigger than "Who dented the car?" or "Why is this project late?" These are issues that are so big, you can't ignore them, blame someone else, or even make an excuse. They're the issues we feel we're not powerful enough to control, like our skills, our intelligence, our appeal to other people. They're the areas where we worry that we're not good enough, strong enough, smart enough, *anything* enough to do what needs to be done to get where we want or need to go. We actually can't imagine how to do it, at least not without suffering in some way.

Except, it's not really *you* telling you you're going to suffer, that you don't measure up and can't possibly do what needs to be done to get what you want.

It's your fear.

This is the level of accountability where fear finally rears its ugly head. It's actually been there all along, hiding behind all those easier justifications for why you failed to do something. But now that you've moved past those, there's nothing left between you and the satisfaction you want so desperately except fear.

This is the moment it takes over and stops you in your tracks.

# Why You Can't Say "I Can't"

Fear was originally designed to help you. It kicks your brain's fight-or-flight response into action, which can really help if, say, a bear is running at you. It's a completely natural response—if you're actually running from a bear, or a fire, or an axe murderer. It's not quite as natural, and far less helpful, if all you need to do is swim fifty meters of the butterfly.

Change is scary. Stepping into the unknown involves taking a risk, which in turn can activate the fear response—even if that risk is something as harmless as being seen doing something less than perfectly, like Salem at that swim meet. And that fear, the fear of looking stupid, can actually be pretty powerful. Most of us have an image we're trying to project to the world, whether it's a physical ability, a mental ability, a level of success, or something else entirely. So when we're facing something new or challenging, fear creeps in and whispers in your ear that you're not good enough, or it's too much to handle. It says you can't.

*It's not really you telling you you're going to suffer, that you don't measure up and can't possibly do what needs to be done to get what you want. It's your fear.*

The problem is, if you listen to fear, it has the power to totally derail you.

When you panic like Salem did, fear clouds your judgment and keeps you from looking for other alternatives. It makes you turn around when you come to that boulder in the middle of your path instead of looking for a toehold, or a place to grab on to, or a ledge to which you can hoist yourself up so you can keep moving forward. Never mind finding another person and helping each other get past it together.

One reason for this is, when faced with a problem, we immediately think about what it will take to solve that problem all at once. It's insisting on eating the "whole elephant" instead of taking it one bite at a time. The problem is, when you reach this level of accountability, despite all the progress you've made, you're actually in a very precarious place. You're not just going to stand there staring at a boulder forever, saying, "I can't go any further because it's too hard for me." It's much easier to turn back and settle into a more comfortable spot, like excuses, or blame ... or even obliviousness.

For example, had Salem not gotten past that moment at the swim meet (we'll get into what happened next in a minute), he probably would have quit the team. He might never have swum again competitively. He would have let that moment define him, and that would have made him a victim.

And again, we get that. We've all been there. We've all given up at one point or another. Because we decide things are too hard when we start to tap the big things in our lives. Those moments where, when we hit a roadblock, we need to push past the fear to move forward. If we don't, we generally tumble back down into the muck and lose all the progress we've made.

For example, imagine you're in a bad marriage. You've tried to ignore the problems. You've gone to counseling. You've tried to change your behavior, your attitude, maybe even how you look. But nothing has made the marriage better. You're miserable, but at the same time, you can't imagine leaving. You're terrified of starting over, of being alone, of what other people will think of you. So you tell yourself you *can't* leave. You've reached the limit of what you can do. You will remain a victim of this bad marriage until death do you part.

When you first make that decision, you're at the It's Too Hard level of accountability, feeling miserable but too scared to do anything about it. But after a while, you might slip back down to excuses when you think about your bad marriage. *I can't give up my lifestyle. It won't be fair to the kids.* Or you might slip even further down the slope, into blame. *I wouldn't be so miserable if my spouse wasn't such a jerk.* You could even fall all the way back to obliviousness, where you deny that there's a problem at all and tell the world, "My marriage is fine," even though you're desperately unhappy. The one sure thing is, no matter how far you fall, your fear will continue to hold you back from experiencing the kind of marriage you want and deserve. Fear will stand between you and a better version of your life.

## So How Do You Get Past That Boulder?

As we mentioned earlier, everyone experiences fear, and because we're all different, we gravitate toward different ways to cope with and move past it. For Salem, that starts with taking some kind of action. It means *doing one thing*, no matter how small, knowing that this one thing may start a trophic cascade that will lead to further action and get you closer to where you ultimately want to go. That's what happened back at that swim meet. His coaches kept yelling, "Jump in!" while he was standing there, frozen like a statue in a Speedo, because they knew that the moment Salem hit the water, something would be familiar again.

And it was.

As soon as he jumped in, he recognized where he was. He was able to tell himself, *Okay, I'll start moving down this lane.* And once he got into something familiar, it felt just like it did at practice. And he was able to finish the butterfly, and the remaining three legs of the IM. Of course he lost—by a lot. The rest of the swimmers were just about on to the backstroke by the time he started moving. But by getting in the water and finishing the race, Salem proved to himself that he *could*. And he never experienced that kind of fear ever again.

So when fear overwhelms you and you have no idea what to do next, or you don't think there's anything you *can* do next, try to pull back and find something—anything—that's familiar. Find that one place to put your foot on the boulder. Find the smallest thing that moves you forward, and start there. Then look for the next little thing, and then the next one. You may fall back down, but so what? It's better than slipping all the way back into the muck. You can learn from your mistakes and try again. Little by little, you can build the skills, knowledge, and/or experience you need to turn "It's too hard" into "I can do it."

Of course, there are situations in life when advice like "Just jump in!" isn't going to be enough. Some of us are wrestling with real trauma, with real pain, with big, serious issues behind our deepest fears. These are the bigger fears, about who we are in the world, and what we deserve, and what we're worthy of. And for Robert, the antidote to that kind of fear is, and always has been, love.

We're not talking about the romantic, huggy, kissy kind of love you find in the movies. We mean the strong, confident, truthful love you find in the people who have your back, like your family, your friends, and God. Just look at how the Bible describes love:

*Love is patient and kind.*

*It's not jealous, proud, or rude.*

*It does not demand its own way.*

*It's not irritable and forgives offenses.*

*It does not rejoice in injustice but rejoices whenever the truth wins out.*

*Love never gives up, never loses faith, is always hopeful, and it endures through every circumstance.*

In other words, we're talking about unconditional love. The unconditional love Robert feels through his relationship with Jesus Christ, as well as his wife and family and friends, gives Robert the strength to face his fears and have the confidence to press on, even when it's hard. Because he knows he will still be loved even if he fails. That frees him to take risks, to push past the fear of change, and find a better life. That kind of faith empowers him to face anything, including (and especially) his deepest fears. That's when he leans on love the hardest.

In a way, Robert's fear was a lot like Salem's at the swim meet. He was also terrified about appearing less than the image he was trying to project to the world, but on a much, much larger and more life-altering scale. But still, the image Robert wanted to present as a business leader included all the traditional trappings of "success"—beginning with his beautiful house. But the reality was, Robert and Kathy couldn't afford that lifestyle, and maintaining it was costing them both financially and psychologically. They were falling deeper and deeper into debt every month they held on to their house.

Robert knew, intellectually, that selling his house was the only way to stop the bleeding. But every time he thought of selling it, his brain immediately told him, *I can't.* How was he supposed to tell people, "Hey, I'm selling my house because I can't keep up with my bills and I've allowed myself to get into debt"? What would everyone think? What about his wife, who worked so hard to create a beautiful home? How could he ask her to sell all that furniture she'd collected and move to a little rental and furnish it with particleboard dressers that would come in boxes for them to put together themselves? Wouldn't that be letting her down?

Those fears kept Robert in that house—and up at night.

But look at it this way. At the very same moment Robert was lying in his bed worrying about how he could hold on to his house and still pay his bills, there were people in war-torn countries unable to find food to eat or water to drink. Refugees who were displaced from their homes and no longer had a roof over their heads. Right now, there are people in this world, including people with children, who actually cannot find a place to sleep.

When you look at it that way, what Robert was facing wasn't that big a deal. He was facing a change in lifestyle. Like Salem jumping in the water, it wasn't going to kill him. This major life crisis was largely over a matter of perspective. Robert was afraid of something that, ultimately, couldn't really hurt him. Not when he was surrounded by the love of God and his wife and family and friends.

But we'll get to that a little later.

## The Power of Other People

Sometimes, changing your perspective and moving past fear is about being able to look beyond your fear to the vision of the life you really want. And sometimes, you need other people to help you do that. You need them to help you see the big picture, or to put that vision together in the first place. That's one big reason Salem was able to jump in the pool and finish the race. He had a coach there to drown out the fear that was telling him, *You can't.*

When you have no idea what to do next, other people can help you get to the other side of the boulder. During one of Robert's CEO group events in Dallas, he hosted a mini version of the Big Dream Gathering designed to help people turn *I can't* into *I can* by getting them to help each other. A group of people come together in a room, and everyone writes their dream down on a piece of paper and hangs it on the wall. Next, everyone walks around the room and looks at everyone else's papers explaining their dreams and writes notes on them. Sometimes the notes are simple encouragement. Sometimes they're specific pieces of advice from people who have had similar experiences. And sometimes, they're actual offers of help.

For example, one guy wrote that his dream was to start a llama farm. One person wrote, *I love llamas. I'll help you.* Another wrote,

*Hey, I got a cousin who owns a bunch of llamas. Let me know if you want to talk.* Another wrote, *I'm a doctor who loves animals, and I'd love to help.* Together, the whole room full of people helped not only this one man pursue his dream—at the same time, they helped everyone in the room pursue theirs.

One word of warning though: while it's helpful to surround yourself with other people, it's important to be selective about the kind of people you surround yourself with. If, when you say, "It's too hard," they say, "You're right," that's the wrong group of people. Having people agree with your fears may feel good in the moment, but it's the last thing you want in the long run. If you were climbing a mountain with Sherpas and you said, "This is really hard. I can't do it," you wouldn't want them to say, "You're right. Let's go back." You'd want them to help you keep moving forward when things got hard. So, if you notice that everybody around you is agreeing with you when you say you can't, it's time to widen your circle of friends and acquaintances and start finding some people who believe in you. You want people around you who will say, "How do I help you push past this? I love you, and I'm here to support you." Those are the people who will help get you past your fear and further up the mountain, where you can finally own it.

## ACCOUNTABILITY EXERCISE: BUILD YOUR OWN DREAM

What could you do, right now, to get past the It's Too Hards that are stopping you from finding true happiness? For this exercise, we're going to replicate some of the processes we saw at the Big Dream Gathering by applying them to the Satisfaction Wheels.

1. Go back to your Satisfaction Wheels and look at those areas where you are dissatisfied. Focus on an area where you have a dream that you have no idea how to make come true.

2. Write your dream down, just like you were writing it down on a piece of paper at the Big Dream Gathering.

3. Think through the steps it will take to bring you closer to your dream. Try to pare down to the smallest step you can take that will get you moving in the right direction.

For example, imagine your dream is to buy a house. What do you need to be able to buy a house? You need money. You need to find the house. You need to know you can afford the house. For that, you'd need to set a budget. Setting a budget is a lot easier than buying a house, so it's a good place to start. And if your budget says you're not going to make it, you can figure out what you need to change—look for a cheaper house, find a way to make more money, wait until you've saved more money to put down ... you can start exploring options.

*The longer you wait to take the first step increases the odds you will never achieve it.*

The cool thing about this exercise is, when you take a step toward addressing a problem, simply taking that step feels so good that it inspires you to take another one. And another one. And pretty soon, you're halfway there. Remember, the longer you wait to take the first step increases the odds you will never achieve it.

So now that you've moved past *I can't,* it's time to tackle the next and final phase at the bottom of the Accountability Mountain—waiting and hoping.

Is this making sense?

Are you seeing how this can help you

live the life you really want?

Tell others about our book.

Take a photo of the book cover and share on

your favorite social media.

Let them know how this is affecting you and

send them to get a copy for themselves at

**www.NobodyCaresBook.com**

# CHAPTER FIVE

## I'll Wait for the Helicopter

*There is no hope.*

—**SALEM THYNE**

Salem was in the UK, working on fixing some issues at one of his company's facilities, when a section of the plant went down. The plant had about forty of these sections, and each one produced about $100,000 worth of product every day. That meant every day this particular section was offline, it cost Salem's company a hundred grand.

This was an old nuclear enrichment plant, built back in the 1950s, and the component that needed to be replaced was an old component. You couldn't just order it online and have Amazon rush it over in an hour or so. Salem's maintenance team had to hunt it down, and after researching where they might find one of those old components, which cost around $25,000, they were able to locate one. They told Salem at that afternoon's staff meeting, saying they would have their replacement component in one week.

Mission accomplished, right?

Not exactly.

If the component arrived when the maintenance guys said it would, this $25,000 part would cost the company $700,000. That seemed crazy. So Salem asked for some clarification. "You're saying it will take *one week* to get this section of the plant back online?"

"Yep," one of the maintenance guys responded. "That's the best we can do."

The best they could do would cost the company $700,000? Again, that didn't seem like the kind of expense a company would just ... swallow. "Explain to me," Salem said. "Does anybody else use this component?"

"Well, yeah ..." one of the guys replied. "It's a standard power component, just basically a battery-backup component. It's kind of old, but I know there's other places that use it."

"Okay ..." Salem responded. "So did you call any of those other plants to see if they have a spare they can loan us, or that we can even buy?"

The guys replied that they had not done that.

So Salem asked, "Where are we getting this component from?"

"Oh," one of the guys said. "Well, we ordered it, but they're going to have to ship it down to us, and they have to get it ready, and there are delays, and they're very busy—"

"Okay," Salem interrupted, "so where's the factory that it's coming from located?"

It was six hours north, in Scotland.

"So," Salem said, "can we drive there and pick it up?"

Silence.

Really, really awkward silence.

Finally, one of the maintenance guys asked, "What do you mean?"

"Can we just drive up there and get it?" Salem asked. "Do they have it in their warehouse?"

"Well," the guy said, "I don't know."

Then the maintenance guys looked at Salem again. "Do you want us to call them?"

They looked at Salem.

They fully expected him to tell them what to do next. That was the only way they could imagine solving this very expensive problem in less than the week that they swore was the best they could do—by waiting for someone else to swoop in like Superman and save the day.

They were stuck at the next level up the Accountability Mountain—Waiting and Hoping.

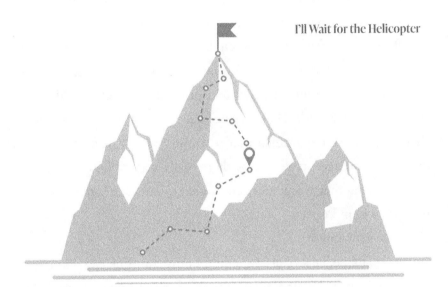

I'll Wait for the Helicopter

## You Are Here

If you're pretty sure you've done everything you can to move ahead in your journey to solve the problem or capture the opportunity, but you're still not getting where you want to be so you're waiting and/or hoping for something to move you across the gap (like a helicopter to swoop in and take you up the Accountability Mountain), it's pretty obvious that you're in Wait and Hope mode. And again, we want to stress that just getting to this point is a major accomplishment. You're not oblivious, you're not blaming others, you're not making excuses, so you've definitely left the muck behind. You've even taken some action. You've *done things,* or in the case of Salem's maintenance team, you've *done a thing*, and as a result, you feel pretty confident that, even though you haven't completely solved the problem, you've done all you can do. You *feel like* you own it.

And you're totally, completely, 100 percent wrong.

You can't call yourself accountable when the things (or thing) you've done are the wrong things. Or you haven't done enough things. Or you haven't done those things the right way. Or the problem still exists. You need to own the outcome—not just the effort.

There's a difference between being *responsible for an action* and being *accountable for the outcome*. Salem's team obviously did something. They found the part and ordered it, which would solve the problem in a week. Had they been accountable for the outcome, they would have determined that that outcome—a likely $700,000 loss—was not acceptable unless there really was no better solution available. And they would have continued to pursue a better solution until they found one.

That's owning it.

In that case, lack of accountability hurt someone else, although of course it hurt the maintenance team's egos and reputations to be called out like that. But waiting and hoping doesn't always have a firm end date, like it did at the plant. Sometimes you wait and hope indefinitely, which has a tendency to turn into *forever*. You try, you put out effort, but you never achieve satisfaction because you don't do enough of the right things to get where you want to go.

Think of the single person who goes on a different online date every other night because they're dying to get married, but they never do, because they never change the behavior that drives every potential partner away. Or the person who wants, needs, and even deserves a raise but never asks for it, waiting and hoping that the boss will finally notice how awesome they are and reward them.

The point is, even if you're the only person who gets hurt, if you're waiting and hoping, you're not reaching satisfaction, and that means you're still not owning it. You're passing it off for someone else to deal with or solve instead of moving it to the point of completion. So you're still not being accountable. You're still in victim mode.

But if it helps, trust us—we've all been there with you.

## Everybody Hopes (and Waits)

If there were a map of the Accountability Mountain, you'd find Waiting and Hoping just a hair above It's Too Hard in the Valley of False Accountability. As we mentioned in the last chapter, these two levels are very similar, linked together in the same way Blame and Excuses are, because they serve the same purpose. Blame and Excuses deflect accountability away from you. Deciding It's Too Hard and Waiting and Hoping stop you from moving forward. You believe you're accountable because you've taken some action, maybe a lot of action, and since you're unable to move forward, you decide that means you're done. Again, you think you've owned it, when you're actually waiting for someone or something else to own it for you.

These two levels are also similar because, when you're there, you tend to get a lot of support from the people around you. Everyone can relate to waiting and hoping. Most people are probably waiting and hoping for something right now! Just think of all the clichés that don't simply justify waiting and hoping, but actually glorify them. *Patience is a virtue. All good things come to those who wait. It's in God's hands now.* As children, we're taught to wait, for things like dessert, and summer vacation, and Christmas. We're taught to wait and hope for what we want.

# So ... What's Wrong with Waiting and Hoping?

Let's get back to the story of Salem at the plant. Because it's not over.

Obviously, when the maintenance guy asked Salem if he "wanted them to call," Salem did. But he also wanted them to figure that out on their own, instead of waiting and hoping for Salem to solve the problem for them by telling them what their next steps were. That was the real problem. They refused to own it. They were practically begging Salem to take the problem off their hands.

This is what people call a "teachable moment." Instead of telling the guys what to do and putting them (and himself) out of their collective misery, Salem asked them, "Well, what can we do? Can you find out more? Have you done everything you can do?"

Because that, right there, is the question at the heart of this whole thing:

*Have you done everything you can do?*

If you haven't, you're either keeping someone else from achieving satisfaction (like Salem's company) or, more often, you're doing it to yourself. Which means you're not owning it, you're not being accountable, and you are being a victim.

By this point, the maintenance guys were pretty embarrassed. Nobody had ever confronted them like that or asked those kinds of questions before. Just ordering something and forgetting about it and going about their normal business was always good enough before. Now, suddenly, the way they had always done things was a problem.

So they said, "Can we get back to you in thirty minutes?"

Salem said, "Sure, we'll meet back in thirty minutes," and thirty minutes later, when they reconvened, the team announced, "We called the place, and they have it in stock. We can actually go pick it up.

So we're going to go pick it up tomorrow afternoon or the day after."

This would have lowered the cost to Salem's company to a few hundred thousand dollars. Was that really the best they could do?

Salem asked the maintenance guys if they could send someone to pick the component up *that night*. Like, ASAP. Once again, the guys were floored that this was even a possibility. "Oh, you mean paying for someone to go up there now … overtime?" Salem reminded them that the component cost $25,000, that every day without the part cost the company $100,000, and that the comparative cost of overtime was so small, so when they did the math …

"Oh," said the maintenance guys. "Well, we didn't know we could do that."

Of course they didn't know—because they didn't think and they didn't ask. They didn't bother to try to find out if there were any solutions that would get the component there in less than a week. They not only planned to wait for the part; once that was revealed to be a problem, they also waited and hoped for someone else to tell them how to get it there faster.

In both cases, *they waited for another person to tell them to do things that they already had the power to do.*

That's what this trap is.

By the way, to end the story, Salem's team sent someone up to Scotland that night, they got back at two in the morning, the guys who did the morning prep installed the component, and the section was up and running six days earlier than it would have been if they had waited and hoped.

Waiting and hoping would have cost them $600,000.

So … what is it costing you?

# The Price of Waiting and Hoping

Things rarely get better when you wait and hope. If you have an infection, and you wait to see the doctor and hope it gets better, chances are it's going to get worse. How often do you hear someone say, "I waited long enough that it worked itself out all by itself. It was amazing!" That doesn't happen, because waiting is not a strategy. It doesn't move you any closer to what you want. And neither does hoping.

They're both placeholders for inaction. They keep you from moving forward.

Then there are those situations where you say you've done everything you can, and you're waiting and hoping for a positive result, but you've really only done everything you *want* to do. Or everything you're comfortable with (remember, comfort zone is just another term for fear). Or everything that comes easily, without putting in too much effort or thought. But not *everything*.

> *Waiting is not a strategy. It doesn't move you any closer to what you want. And neither does hoping. They're both placeholders for inaction. They keep you from moving forward.*

Robert experienced this with his debt problem. Every year, he and his wife said, "Hey, next year will be a better year for us financially." They did everything they (thought they) could and then waited and hoped for the business to take off. But the business kept not taking off, and while they were waiting and hoping, they kept sinking further and further into debt. They weren't getting any closer to satisfaction—instead, it was slipping further and further away. However, while Robert knew that selling the house and paying off his debt was a possible way out, he also didn't want to.

It basically came down to a choice between two things Robert didn't want. He didn't want to sell their house and start over. But he also didn't want to be in debt and have the plaguing, haunting feeling that he was never going to get out of it. Ultimately, he just had to answer that one, simple question. *Which one do you want?*

Did he want to keep doing the thing that wasn't working, or did he want peace of mind?

The thing is, if you're desperate, that's never a question. You don't worry about what you want. If you're starving, you don't turn down a bowl of mush because you'd rather have pizza. If there's no roof over your head, you don't care what neighborhood the roof is in. You'll do anything and everything to fix the situation. You'll eat anything, you'll take any job, you'll do anything.

So the next time you catch yourself waiting and hoping, ask yourself this question: "Have I done everything I *want* to do, or everything I actually *can* do?"

Because those are often two very different things.

# Beyond Waiting and Hoping

There are times in life when you really do have to wait. But there's a difference between waiting and *actively* waiting. Actively waiting embraces the fact that you still have a role in the outcome, so there are still things you can do to move yourself closer to your goal while you wait to achieve it. It's like going to college. You have to wait to graduate, but that doesn't mean you just sit there hoping to get a degree. Robert had to (actively) wait for his business to grow and relieve his financial burdens, but he still had to work very hard to find new business while also serving and keeping all the clients he had.

But even that level of active waiting didn't make his stress go away. For that to happen, he needed to make even bigger changes, even if it meant doing something he didn't want to do. In other words, waiting doesn't mean sitting around until someone else does it for you. It's still on you. You still need to own it.

As for hoping, hope alone never got anyone anywhere. Hoping something happens has absolutely no bearing on the outcome. Which brings us to the quote from Salem at the beginning of this chapter. He was still working with that team in the UK, continuing to push them to be more accountable by asking the same kinds of questions about whether they were really doing the best they could do, when he came up with a catchphrase that eventually became the mantra at the site: "There Is No Hope." Because when Salem removed the word *hope* from everyone's vocabulary—which we know sounds like we're getting all *Star Wars* again, but bear with us—things changed.

Look what happens when you eliminate that word. *We're hoping to get the part today.* No, you call and find it and confirm, and you ask, "Do you know where the driver is?" and "Do you have a tracking code?" And you *make sure* you get the part today. It's the difference between sitting and waiting for the thing to show up and following the driver on their route online until the thing you need is in your hands.

It's okay to *have* hope for things, like world peace, or a cure for cancer, or that your team will win the Super Bowl. But it's not enough to hope *for* things, like success, romance, or peace. You have to go out and get them. That's how you own it.

It works the same way with prayer. We're both Christians, so we both believe in the power of prayer. But, for a lot of people, prayer works kind of like hope. There's a famous story about a man and a flood. A horrible storm comes and floods this guy's house, so he climbs up on the roof of his house and prays, "Oh, God. Help me. Help me." All of a sudden, a boat comes by, and the captain says, "Get in the boat." And the man on the roof says, "No, I'm praying to God. He's got me covered." The water gets higher and higher, and when it reaches the roof, the guy starts to panic. He says, "Lord, where are you? Come on. Help me." And a helicopter shows up, and the pilot says, "Get in." But the guy on what's left of the roof says, "No, I'm praying to God. I'm praying to God." And the water keeps rising, and the guy drowns in the flood and

*It's okay to have hope for things, like world peace, or a cure for cancer, or that your team will win the Super Bowl. But it's not enough to hope for things, like success, romance, or peace. You have to go out and get them. That's how you own it.*

goes to heaven. And when he gets there, he looks at God and says, "Where were you that whole time?" And God says, "Dude, I sent you a boat and a helicopter. What's your problem?"

Honestly, letting go of hope isn't an easy thing to do. It took Salem's team a full year to get the word *hope* out of their language at the plant. But when it happens, when you finally move beyond hope, you start to do things. You start to take ownership. And you start to see results and move closer to satisfaction.

So, how can you make sure you're being proactive and doing, and not reverting to passive waiting and hoping as you climb the Accountability Mountain? One way is to revisit what you're doing and ask yourself, "Is this enough?"

Hint—the answer is (almost) always no.

It reminds us of a story from the autobiography of former president Jimmy Carter, who was, like Salem, a part of the nuclear navy. Before his campaign for president back in the 1970s, he released the book titled *Why Not the Best?*, a line taken from a conversation he'd had with Admiral Hyman Rickover. The navy legend was interviewing Carter for a job with America's nuclear submarine program. As Carter related in the book, "It was the first time I met Admiral Rickover, and we sat in a large room by ourselves for more than two hours. He let me choose any subjects I wished to discuss. Very carefully, I chose those about which I knew the most about at the time—current events, seamanship, music, literature, naval tactics, electronics, gunnery—and he began to ask me a series of questions of increasing difficulty. In each instance, he soon proved that I knew relatively little about the subject I had chosen. He always looked right into my eyes and never smiled. I was saturated with cold sweat."

Finally, Rickover asked the man who would one day be his commander in chief, the future president of the United States, "Did you do your best?"

Carter writes, "I started to say 'Yes, sir.' But I remembered who this was, and I recalled several times I could have learned more about our allies, our enemies, weapons, strategy, so forth. I was just human. I finally gulped and said, 'No, sir, I didn't always do my best.' He looked at me for a long time and then turned his chair around to end the interview. He asked one final question, which I have never been able to forget, or to answer.

"He said, 'Why not?'

"I sat there for a while, shaken, and then slowly left the room."

Yes, we realize we're talking about a conversation between two of the most consequential, powerful men in the world. But at some level, the same question applies to all of us. Why not the best? Why would you deprive yourself of the life you really want when you don't have to?

And even after you achieve that, why would you stop? You want to continue to have goals and take action toward those goals, to keep yourself moving. Because the bad thing about waiting and hoping is that, when you get stuck at this level, you never go any further. Whatever you've done, if it hasn't solved the problem, it's not enough, so it's not going to. If you're not happier, you're not changing, you're not content, then you're not *done*. And that means you're not accountable.

And maybe you truly don't know. Maybe you actually can't see the places in your life where you haven't done all you can, where you're not being accountable even though you think you are. That brings us back to the Satisfaction Wheel for our next exercise.

 # ACCOUNTABILITY EXERCISE: SHARE YOUR STORY

In this exercise, you are going to invite someone you really, really trust—a friend, your spouse, a coach or counselor—to look at your Satisfaction Wheels and comment on them. Think of it as a kind of reality check.

Show your Satisfaction Wheels to this trusted person and explain how they work and what they represent. Tell them how the numbers on your wheels represent your sense of where you are today, what your life looks like, and how you feel about it. You can even talk about the work you've been doing with the wheels and some of the ideas you have about moving forward.

Remember to be honest and be vulnerable, because being vulnerable is the only way you can get better. Be honest about where you think you are, and then be equally honest about why you believe your satisfaction level is where it is. Then ask the person, "What do you think?" Invite them to share their own thoughts about what you're doing in each of these areas, and ask if they have any ideas about how you might bring those satisfaction levels up. Encourage them to be brutally honest—make sure they know the whole point of this exercise is to help you see what you can't see on your own. Because that can also help you own it.

You've done a lot of work to reach this level on the Accountability Mountain, and in the next chapter, it's going to begin to pay off—when we Cross the Ravine and finally take our first step toward true accountability.

Is this making sense?
Are you seeing how this can help you
live the life you really want?
Tell others about our book.
Take a photo of the book cover and share on
your favorite social media.
Let them know how this is affecting you and
send them to get a copy for themselves at

**www.NobodyCaresBook.com**

# CHAPTER SIX

## Crossing the Ravine

*You will make a change when the pain of staying where you are is worse than the pain of where you are going.*

## —ROBERT HUNT

It took a lot for Robert to finally put his house on the market. In fact, his journey to that monumental decision took him halfway up the Accountability Mountain.

When Robert's troubles started, he was just launching his business. Everyone says you have to spend money to make money, so that's what Robert did, and while he was sinking deeper and deeper into debt, he didn't really focus on it. He was oblivious to the problem until it got so big it started causing him pain. Then he had to pay attention. And when he realized he was in trouble, he started looking for the *reason*.

We've already established that this is normal human nature. When something happens, our brains want to know *why*. So Robert's brain went to work to explain his predicament. First, he blamed the economy. But when he looked around and saw a lot of other businesspeople he knew who seemed to be doing just fine, he realized that wasn't true. And blaming the economy didn't solve the problem. So he found an excuse for why he wasn't doing as well as those other businesspeople—he sucked at sales.

That didn't solve the problem either. Instead, it got worse. Robert sunk even deeper into debt. Blame and excuses weren't getting him anywhere. He had to do *something*. So he read some books, worked on some different sales techniques, and tried to improve as a salesman. But his bank balance didn't go up. His debt did. Still, while Robert hadn't solved the problem, he decided that he had done all he could. After all, he had gotten better at sales, and he was still in debt. That meant he could only wait and hope for things to get better ...

And pretty soon, Robert owed $90,000.

Robert and Kathy knew, at their current rate of income, it would take years to pay off that amount of debt. That was why they began to explore the option of selling their house and starting over in the first place. But they really hoped they wouldn't have to take it that far. It was crazy, right? You don't sell your *house* just because your business hasn't taken off yet ... do you? It was so much easier for Robert to keep doing what he was doing and waiting and hoping for something to change.

And something did change. He got vertigo.

You've probably heard the term *vertigo*, but you may not know exactly what it is, except an old Hitchcock movie. MedicineNet defines it as "a feeling that you are dizzily turning around or that things are dizzily turning about you" and lists potential causes as inner ear and vision problems.[11] The National Institutes of Health have also linked vertigo to psychiatric conditions, including anxiety.[12] Which, as it turned out, was the cause of Robert's bout with the condition.

Robert's vertigo lasted sixteen days. And it shook him. Clearly,

---

11    Melissa Conrad Stöppler, MD, "Medical Definition of Vertigo," *MedicineNet,* March 29, 2021, https://www.medicinenet.com/vertigo/definition.htm.

12    "Anxiety, Mood, and Personality Disorders in Patients with Benign Paroxysmal Positional Vertigo," US National Library of Medicine, National Institutes of Health, https://www.ncbi.nlm.nih.gov/pmc/articles/PMC6045803/.

waiting and hoping wasn't working. There was no way he was going to grow his business while he was feeling so sick, so what exactly was he waiting and hoping for? He started wondering, *What if my life is going to be like this forever? I'm screwed.* As long as he kept doing what he was doing, there was no way his life was ever going to change.

First, he ran through his by then well-worn, default list of *reasons* he was in this predicament. He worked his way up from the bottom of the mountain in his mind, justifying why his business wasn't bringing in the money he needed it to, why it was okay for him to carry so much debt, how he had been working so hard, how some people are just luckier than others and better at sales, and how maybe God didn't want him to grow his business any further ... and all of a sudden it all hit him ...

It was all BS.

Nobody cared!

Nobody cared about his lame excuses for why he was where he was that day.

Nobody cared if he was in debt or not, or why he was in debt, or what he had or had not done to help his business, or if his business was a success, or how much money God wanted him to make. Nobody cared that he was struggling with a mountain of stress that was even bigger than his mountain of debt. Nobody cared that he had been working his butt off for six years and still only had a few clients.

They all had their own problems.

Salem had the same kind of epiphany years earlier, when he left the military and came home to his wife and two kids ... and learned his life wasn't at all what he thought it was. His wife was having an affair, wasn't happy, and flat out did not want to be with him. She moved out of state with their kids, who were seven and two. And suddenly, Salem's life, which had been completely planned, where he understood everything he was going to do, where he was 100 percent sure he was heading toward glory and fame and fortune and happiness with this family that he thought he would have for the rest of his life, was over.

So Salem decided to turn that metaphor into reality.

He had so much hurt and pain he didn't know what to do. He blamed everything and anybody—the military, his soon-to-be-ex-wife, himself for not being home more and for choosing the military lifestyle. He started drinking to numb the pain, and then he added drugs to numb it a little more.

On some level, he was punishing himself. He felt he deserved it.

And after being in a place of 100 percent accountability in the military, Salem fell right off the mountain, all the way to the bottom, to self-imposed obliviousness. And instead of trying to climb back up, he set up camp there. It was as if he said, "Oh yeah, let's see how bad I can make it" and then promptly rose to the challenge. He blew money, drank, did drugs, did everything he possibly could to put himself in the worst possible place. And pretty soon, he found himself there—alone in his apartment making the decision to try to drink himself to death. With some help from some painkillers.

Salem saw it like this: If he didn't wake up the next day, his problems would be solved. If he did happen to wake up the next day, he had to stop doing what he was doing. It was almost like he took his life and said, "One way or the other, I've made a decision here." Almost like he was daring God to take him.

And wouldn't you know it? He woke up.

He woke up in a pile of boxes, with no idea where he was. Following this epic dark night of the soul, there were no texts on his phone. Nobody called and asked, "Hey, how're you doing?"

Nobody cared.

He was miserable, he had just tried to kill himself, his life was a mess, and nobody cared.

And guess what? Whatever stories you've been telling yourself about why you are where you are, and why you don't have what you want, and why things can't possibly change ... nobody cares about those either. Harsh—but true.

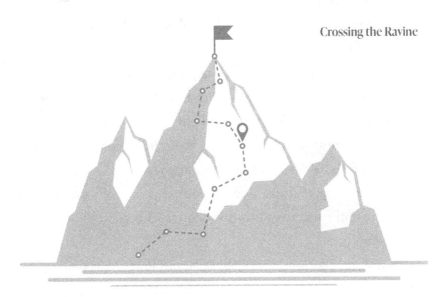

Crossing the Ravine

## You Are Here

Right now, you've reached the turning point in the journey. It's not a boulder in the middle of the path. It's like reaching the edge of a cliff. And the only way across to where you want to go is like a rickety ladder across a crevasse on Mount Everest.

The only way is to take a leap of faith.

When you come face to face with the fact that nothing you're doing is working—if you want to move forward, if you want the pain to stop, if you want to finally get where you want to go—you're going to have to do the hardest thing you've ever done.

You're going to have to let go of your fear and take a leap of faith.

And if you're going to do that, you have to be ready.

So—are you?

Are you ready to face down whatever it is you're most afraid of—the thing that scares you so much you can't even imagine looking at it?

If not, we have a gentle suggestion for you.

Put this book down.

Seriously. Just put it down. We won't know. We won't care.

Nobody cares.

No, not because nobody cares about you as a human being. We wrote this book because we care—a lot, actually. But when it comes to the story you've been telling yourself about why you are where you are, about why nothing works out for you, about how you're just unlucky and doomed and a victim, *that's* where nobody cares.

Nobody cares that you grew up poor or your mother didn't love you or the traffic was terrible or the dog ate your homework.

*Nobody cares.*

Seriously. Take a moment and say it out loud, right now:

*Nobody cares.*

Sit with that for a while. Really let it sink in.

# NOBODY CARES.

So, what are those things you've been telling yourself, and the rest of the world, that nobody cares about? Think back to those *reasons* you're not satisfied. What's the one thing you find yourself saying over and over to justify your situation? Your *my-mommy-didn't-love-me-I-grew-up-poor-I'm-just-unlucky* or whatever you tell yourself when you feel like crap?

Write that down.

Then say those two magic words:

*Nobody cares.*

Now write down every single area in your life where you're not satisfied, where you're not performing, where things aren't the way you want them to be. Write down all those things you think are holding you back, from *My boss is a jerk* to *I'm a procrastinator* to *Traffic was a nightmare*. Write down the *reasons* for all your problems, all your sadness, all your disappointment, all your pain. Look at your Satisfaction Wheels, at all the areas where you aren't where you want to be, and at the excuses you have for being where you are, and add those to the list.

And next to each of them, write those two words:

*Nobody cares.*

When you're done, you should have a pretty exhaustive list of the excuses and blame and reasons that have been holding you back.

And also a clear indication of exactly who gives a crap.

Which brings us to the final part of this exercise.

At the bottom of your list, write three more words:

*Until I do.*

Now we want you to stop.

Put this book down for a while, and sit with that thought. Take a walk. Sleep on it. When you're really ready to take that leap of faith, we'll be waiting for you on the other side.

Is this making sense?
Are you seeing how this can help you
live the life you really want?
Tell others about our book.
Take a photo of the book cover and share on
your favorite social media.
Let them know how this is affecting you and
send them to get a copy for themselves at

**www.NobodyCaresBook.com**

# PART II

## The View From Above

You did it.

You took the leap. You crossed the ravine. You are now, officially, ready to climb the Accountability Mountain. You're ready to own it.

But in many ways, this is just the beginning of your journey.

The first half of this process has been about getting you past the things that have been holding you back and keeping you down. Look back across the ravine, and you can see all of them—the fog of obliviousness, the muck of blame and excuses, the boulder that was too hard to pass, and the edge of the ravine where you waited and hoped for something to carry you across ...

Until you took that leap of faith toward the life you want and left everything holding you back.

Now we can get to work.

Over the next, final chapters, you will find the tools to take your quest for accountability as far as it can go—and then just a little bit further. You'll build the muscles you need to scale the highest peaks and get closer and closer to your goals. But before you can do that, before you can reach peak accountability, you have to do the thing you've been avoiding all your life. You really, truly have to own it. And in order to do that, you need to do the hardest, scariest thing you will ever do.

You need to face reality.

# CHAPTER SEVEN

## Start the Climb

*Our deepest fear is not that we're inadequate. Our deepest fear is that we're powerful beyond measure.*

## —MARIANNE WILLIAMSON

In case you're wondering, the title of this chapter is not a misprint. You may have been on this journey with us for a hundred pages or so, but in terms of where you're headed, this is actually just base camp. As long as fear was holding you down, you couldn't really rise very high above all the head trash on the other side of the ravine. Now, you can see the mountain in front of you.

And you see just how far you still have to go.

We know it's a little overwhelming. We've been there. But we promise you … it's also doable.

If you were actually at base camp, looking up at the peak of Mount Everest, you'd probably have a similar reaction. Your immediate thought would probably be something along the lines of *Holy crap, how can I ever possibly get up there?* The task is too big to process all at once. You need to break it down into manageable steps. And the very first step is figuring out where you are. Only then can you assess how far you have to go, how long it will take to climb to the top, where it's safe to make camp along the way, what challenges you're likely to face, and whether you're up to those challenges. All of those things comprise your reality. And until you acknowledge that reality, you can't move forward.

So that's what this chapter is all about.

## Reality versus *Your* Reality

If there was one thing Salem knew about himself, it was that he was definitely, absolutely, positively *not* racist. How could he be? His best friend for around fifteen years, who was more like a brother than a friend, was (and still is!) a Black guy. Clearly, Salem didn't think he was better than or deserved more than his own best friend, whom he hung out with regularly. He *couldn't* be racist. That was just reality.

Then the George Floyd murder happened, and Black Lives Matter protests rocked the country, and suddenly a lot of white people were talking about racism in ways we hadn't before. Pundits and academics debated issues like systemic racism and whether a person could be racist without even realizing it, and Salem started wondering … *Could what they were saying possibly apply to me?*

It didn't seem likely, but it was important enough to Salem and his view of himself as a nonracist to take a personal inventory. He decided to test his accountability around the issue of racism and find out if his actual reality matched his idea of reality.

The first red flag for Salem was the way he tensed up whenever he heard the term *white privilege*. To be honest, it really pissed him off. He grew up poor with divorced parents—a recovering alcoholic mother and a father who, despite that PhD, *still* had to struggle to pay the bills. He lived in apartments in the worst neighborhoods you can imagine, he drank government milk and ate government cheese, and he didn't even graduate high school! Where the hell was *his* privilege?

So when Salem heard terms like *economic disparity*, he called BS. It's not like his family had "generational wealth." Nobody ever gave him a handout or a leg up. He started at the bottom and worked his ass off to get where he was. Everything he had, everything he'd built, he'd done on his own, with no help from anybody.

But this all happened at a point when Salem was already pretty high up the Accountability Mountain. He'd been challenging himself and his reality in other areas and saw himself as a person who held himself to a higher standard. If he was really going to question the reality of his nonracism, that meant going deeper than knee-jerk emotional responses and taking a hard look at the facts.

Salem went back through his history, retracing his steps from high school dropout, or at least nongraduate, to successful CEO. He thought back to his first jobs at restaurants and bars—the only kinds of jobs a person without a high school diploma can get. Salem remembered he worked his butt off at those jobs, and all the jobs that came afterward, and that's how he was able to get noticed and rise through the ranks. His success came from hard work, so he assumed he deserved it. After all, nobody had handed it to him.

But were those *all* the relevant facts? Was it only about Salem's work ethic and ability to impress the higher-ups? Or was it also about those higher-ups? He asked himself, "Who interviewed me for every job I ever applied to? What did they look like?"

Surprise!

Every single one of them was white.

In fact, thinking back over his entire career, Salem couldn't remember a time when he was interviewed by someone who didn't look or talk a lot like him.

That was the moment Salem acknowledged reality. If he planned to continue to view himself as a nonracist, he needed to take all those things he didn't see into account and incorporate them into his life moving forward.

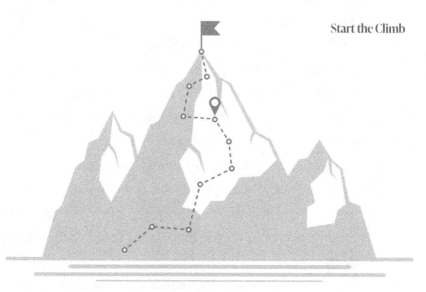

Start the Climb

# You Are Here

If you're like most of us, you're probably pretty sure you know what reality is. You tell yourself the occasional story, maybe you lie to yourself once in a while, but you assume that, if for some reason you needed to accurately define your reality right now, you could do it pretty easily.

You would be wrong.

Until you learn how to look at yourself 100 percent objectively, the way Salem did around racism, you only know *your* reality. And your reality is just a jumbled mix of junk that you developed beginning when you were a child. Thanks to the way your family saw the world and the things you were punished or rewarded for, you learned to make excuses for and explain things to make sense of the world around you. We call these things filters, because they distort the way you see reality. Because your brain always wants to know *why,* those filters help provide the *reasons* that shape the way you see things. The older you've gotten and the more you've experienced, the more of those filters you've applied to your reality.

A filter can be as small as the fact that you didn't sleep well one night. The following day, that filter of "I didn't sleep last night" can provide reasons for just about anything, from being late to work, to snapping at a coworker, to missing a deadline. The problem is, reality doesn't need a reason or explanation. It just *is*. You were late to work. You snapped at a coworker. You missed a deadline. That's reality. The filters providing the "reasons" for that reality wind up distorting it until you don't even know what's real and what isn't. And how can you own it if you don't even know what "it" is?

The only way to get rid of the filters is to stand in front of a (metaphorical) 360-degree mirror and face the real, ugly truth of your life.

Looking in that mirror, with no filters, with no explanations, with no excuses, is that "hardest thing you'll ever do" that we've been warning you about. If you've ever stood naked in front of a real 360-degree mirror, you know it's not always the most pleasant experience. That's why, most of the time, most of us avoid that mirror like the plague so we don't have to look at the parts of ourselves we don't want to see.

However, just because you don't look at them doesn't mean they don't exist.

In fact, the simple fact that you don't look at those parts, while you might not think much about them, means you've actually grown comfortable with them. Like the twenty extra pounds you

*The only way to get rid of the filters is to stand in front of a (metaphorical) 360-degree mirror and face the real, ugly truth of your life.*

may be lugging around because *that's just the way my body is.* Or the debt that keeps you up at night. Or the marriage that isn't working. They've become part of who you are and how you operate in the world. And the really insidious part? Part of the reason you've held on to them for so long is that they've shielded you from your fear.

But what are you really afraid of?

We started this chapter with that quote from Marianne Williamson for a reason. Are we really afraid of not being good enough? Or are we afraid of the awesome responsibility that would come with owning our power and being as great as we can be? That's what makes this the scariest part of this journey. You're leaping into the unknown here. In a sense, you don't know where this might take you.

That 360-degree mirror might reveal the secret to your greatness. It's also going to reveal your flaws, including flaws you had no idea you have. Everything about you that you can't, won't, or don't see is in that mirror, and those things comprise your actual reality. So all looking in that mirror really means is acknowledging where things aren't working so well so you can fix them and make them better.

For example, when Salem challenged himself about racism, he saw past his filters, like that he grew up poor, or that his best friend was Black, or that he worked his butt off, and saw the reality of his privilege. And okay, learning this about himself probably wasn't the scariest thing in Salem's life. But a lot of times, our filters prevent us from seeing bigger things that stand in the way of our actual happiness and well-being.

Accepting reality without filters is so crucial to moving forward in life, it's the very first step in the program *Stanford Medicine* calls the "most effective path to alcohol abstinence,"[13] Alcoholics Anonymous. When you go to an AA meeting, the first thing you have to do if you want to participate is acknowledge that you are an alcoholic.

*Because you have to admit there's a problem before you can solve a problem.*

That's true on this journey, or any journey. You have to know where you are to figure out what you need to do to get where you want to go. How can you make a plan if you don't even know where you're starting?

Still, we resist seeing the whole truth of where that starting point is, because we're afraid of what it will do to us. We're afraid we won't be able to handle the truth—that it will somehow destroy us. Which, when you think about it, is crazy, right? We're living in reality right now, even if we can't see it. Why is seeing the world and ourselves for what they are such a terrifying thing? What exactly are we protecting ourselves from?

# Facing the Fear Monster

Sometimes, our filters are actually protecting us from something really, truly horrible. Take Salem's mother, for instance. She was sexually assaulted at a very young age by family members and other people she trusted. So she had more than a few filters in place to help her survive. She suffered all sorts of issues throughout her life and along the way went through all sorts of treatment. And do you know what finally enabled her to break through and get past her pain?

Not talking about the reasons it happened.

---

13   Mandy Erickson, "Alcoholics Anonymous most effective path to alcohol abstinence," *Stanford Medicine News Center,* March 11, 2020, https://med.stanford.edu/news/all-news/2020/03/alcoholics-anonymous-most-effective-path-to-alcohol-abstinence.html.

Not pondering what could have happened differently.

Not discussing why what happened was so terrible.

It was the simple act of admitting it happened.

Victim advocacy experts will tell you, the first step to healing is acknowledging that it happened—not why it happened or who did it, just acknowledging the fact that it happened.

This isn't an easy thing to do. We have to trick our brain to move past the filters that are protecting us from pain and say, "You know what? This happened." When Robert decided to face the truth about his finances, he had to stop thinking about the economy and whether or not he was good at sales and whether or not he was a failure and what people might think of him and focus on the scariest thing in the world: the numbers on his bank balance and credit card and loan statements. He had to face the cold, hard reality that he was $90,000 in debt.

It was a terrifying moment. Without the unconditional love he felt from God and Kathy and the friends who supported him, he might not have felt strong enough to look. And honestly, the moment he stood there naked and saw his life for what it was, it felt like a punch in the gut. But guess what else it did? By forcing Robert to face reality, it showed him where he actually was. And once he saw it, he could finally, truly own it.

That freed Robert to make a plan to move forward.

He could finally begin to move from victim to victor.

Those bank statements were Robert's 360-degree mirror. Numbers don't lie, so they were able to provide Robert with a clear, irrefutable picture of his reality. (By the way, being able to make the minimum payments on your credit card does not mean you have things under control. Just FYI.) However, sometimes you don't have something as black and white as a list of numbers to look at. Sometimes, there are aspects of your reality you really, genuinely can't see, no matter how hard you look. That's when it can help to turn to other people to help you see what you're not seeing. But it's important to approach these people in the right way—we'll get to that a little further up the mountain.

For now, just taking this step, finally looking in that 360-degree mirror and acknowledging your reality, is enough. Because it's freakin' hard! We know, because we've both done it, multiple times. But we also know that this one step is absolutely, totally, completely life changing. Because once you face reality, you can finally do something about it. You can move past waiting and hoping and blame and excuses and reasons and all the other filters and focus on the only thing that matters—what happens *next*.

## Okay ... So What Does Happen Next?

When you finally do the scariest thing you can possibly do and look in that 360-degree mirror and face reality, you may experience some strong emotions. You may cry. You may collapse—especially if it's something especially painful, like what happened to Salem's mom. Or, depending on your personality or how much of your reality you've kind of already accepted, you may not fall apart or even feel especially bad. Just know that you will, in some fashion, feel that thing you've been avoiding because you're afraid to feel it because you think it will be so horrible it will kill you.

> *Once you face reality, you can finally do something about it. You can move past waiting and hoping and blame and excuses and reasons and all the other filters and focus on the only thing that matters— what happens next.*

And you won't die—no matter how bad it is.

In fact, you can finally start to heal.

You have to acknowledge the problem to fix it, remember? All the other stuff is just Band-Aids on a bullet wound, which isn't going to do anything. Whereas when you actually acknowledge a bullet wound, you can start to work from there. For the first time, you really can have hope. Because the hope will be real. Things can finally get better, because you finally know where you are.

In our experience, the moment you finally acknowledge reality, your happiness goes up instantaneously. When you're no longer in conflict and your brain isn't struggling to paper over the problem with this filter or that one, and you've identified the problem, you are finally free to figure out a solution.

Solutions are different to different people. Acknowledging the reality of a situation also involves acknowledging the steps it will take to change it, and sometimes, for whatever reason, when you balance where you are with what it will take to get where you want to go, you may not be ready or willing to do those things. Say you know you need to lose twenty pounds and that this is your reality, but you also know that losing those twenty pounds will mean making lifestyle changes you don't want to make. As long as you accept the reality that you are twenty pounds overweight, you own it. You can't be mad at the twenty pounds—they're just pounds! You can decide on your own what, if anything, you want to do about them. You're free to pursue victory, whatever that looks like to you.

That's what's so powerful about accepting reality. It may be the hardest, most painful thing you'll ever do, but it's also the most significant. Because it instantly moves you from victim to victor by putting you in control of what happens next.

# ACCOUNTABILITY EXERCISE: FINDING REALITY

Today, we're going to go back to your Satisfaction Wheels and pick out an area where you're not satisfied. Again, start with one that's really nagging at you, knowing you'll move into the other areas later.

Think about that area of dissatisfaction, and ask yourself, "Why?" Write down everything that comes to mind. For example, if you're dissatisfied with finances, write down all the "reasons," like *everything is so expensive!* Or, *I don't make enough money!*

Now go back through your list and get rid of any reasons that are filters, like excuses or explanations. These are the lies you've told over and over, to yourself and to others, so often that you have to reset them. Eventually, you'll get to the reality of your situation. "I have $10 in my bank account." That's your reality. Let that sink in. None of the "whys" or "becauses." Just, "I have $10 in my bank account."

That may be the first time you ever speak the truth to yourself.

So, go make more money, or spend less.

And just like that, you've started moving from victim to victor. Be proud of yourself.

In the next chapter, we'll continue our climb by moving from acknowledging reality to actually accepting it.

# CHAPTER EIGHT

## I Can See the Valley Below

*Don't look back—you're not going that way.*

—MARY ENGELBREIT

Once Robert and Kathy faced reality, there was really no question as to what they had to do. When they did the math, there was only one solution to their problem of constantly escalating bills and constantly escalating stress. They needed to sell their house.

And that was going to suck.

After all, Robert and Kathy's house wasn't just a house—it was their *home,* and it was perfect for the life they had dreamed of and planned for. It was big and beautiful, spanning thirty-five hundred square feet, with four bedrooms, a huge office, a massive backyard, and even an oversized garage with room for all of Robert and James's toys. But the best part was the movie theater upstairs. It had a giant screen and those big, movie-theater chairs that recline. Robert and Kathy loved hanging out in that theater with James, inviting friends and family over, watching movies together.

That was what that house meant to them. It was a haven for Robert and Kathy and the people they cared about. When Kathy furnished the house, she was creating the destination for big family gatherings like Christmas and Thanksgiving—the dining table could seat twenty people! Around the table, they had these beautiful, regal chairs that made Robert feel like a king every time he sat in one.

And now they had to let it all go. Wherever they were going, a home theater with a giant screen and a dining table for twenty were not going to fit. Robert couldn't remember what they paid for it, but they sold it for like $300. That sucked.

They also sold the chairs, and the movie-theater chairs, and the oversized couches, and just about everything they had loved and treasured and snuggled on over the six years they'd spent living in that house. There was no room for any of it in their new rental, except their beds and dressers.

It really, really sucked.

But do you know what sucked more? Living in constant stress. Getting vertigo. Waiting and hoping for something to finally break his way while everything got worse and worse.

So Robert made a decision. He decided he would rather live in a tiny rented house with the woman he loved than in a giant, luxurious home with all the stress and strain they'd been living with coming between them.

That was the day Robert stopped fighting reality and embraced the suck.

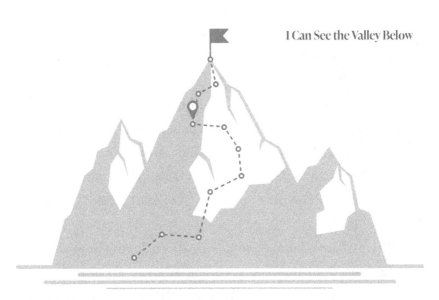

# You Are Here

There's a point on this climb up the Accountability Mountain that will bring you to your knees. A point where you're pulling yourself up and your hands are getting cut from the rocks and you're miserably tired, and you start to think, *Why am I doing this? Maybe it's not worth it.*

This is the part of your journey where you need to reach a decision. If you want to continue to move forward, or even stay where you are, you're going to have to do something we haven't really dealt with yet in this book. You're going to have to *work*.

You definitely don't have to attack every single problem in your life at the same time (and we strongly suggest starting with one thing). You don't even have to climb any higher if you don't want to. From this point forward on your journey, it's okay to choose to stay where you are, because you've moved from being a victim to owning your life. But if you decide to continue to scale the mountain in front of you, you need to Embrace the Suck.

Which means … what, exactly?

At the last level, you looked in that scary 360-degree mirror and saw the thing you didn't want to see. You acknowledged reality. Unfortunately, while acknowledging reality is one thing, it's a whole other thing not to turn away after the shock of seeing the thing you've been avoiding. This is the level where your reality lives, so if you're going to stay here, that means embracing that reality and reveling in it and fully, totally, and completely immersing yourself in it. That's not just looking your fear in the face—it's standing up to it and telling fear to get lost!

That's what we mean by embracing the suck. And we're not going to sugarcoat this in any way. It's freakin' *hard*.

It was hard for Robert and Kathy to sell their furniture for pennies on the dollar. It was hard for them to walk away from a house that represented all of their dreams and six years of their lives. But they did it. They embraced the reality that they could not afford to own that house, or any house, while they were $90,000 in debt. So they let it go, furniture and all, and gave themselves over to the experience of living in their new reality.

Which, to be honest, was their only reality.

Embracing the suck is the harsh reality check that's necessary if you're going to make a change. It's throwing away the filters that have explained or excused or obscured or prettied up your situation and finally saying, "This is who and where and what I am." It's giving up that constant struggle to define your situation as something other than what it is (i.e., *not your fault*) and embracing your position or place in life—whatever it entails, however sucky it may be. It's the painful side of owning it, the side that says, "Whatever isn't working in your life, it's all on you." But if you can't do that, not only will you not move any further up the mountain—you risk slipping back down.

# Why You Need to Love the Suck

"Embrace the Suck" is a mantra in the military. Salem picked it up at boot camp—which, even if you've never been to boot camp, you know from movies and TV is all about putting soldiers through an escalating series of things that suck. You know, the long runs in the rain, endless push-ups in hundred-degree heat, the drill sergeant screaming obscenities and insults in your face ... things like that. Not to be abusive—the military treats its recruits like crap for a very good reason. Soldiers need to be ready to go to war, and trying to kill people before they kill you is pretty much the pinnacle of suck. If you're going to survive that, never mind the thirteen weeks of organized torture designed to get you ready to survive that, you can't fight your reality. You have to give yourself over to it and say, "I'm going to love it."

That's what Salem did at boot camp. He gave himself over to the reality of his experience. He told himself, "I'm going to love that my feet are bleeding every morning, because I have such bad athlete's foot, and we're not allowed to get treatments. I'm going to love the fact that my pink eye is so bad I can't open my eyes. I'm going to love it and I'm going to embrace it, because that's the only way I can move forward and get to the other side of this."

And after thirteen weeks, he did. By embracing the suck, he survived the suck.

Embracing the suck is so fundamental to moving forward in life, it even works in nature. For example, look at the contrast between buffalo (which are wild) and cattle (which are domesticated) and how they behave when a storm is coming. When cattle see a storm, they panic. They don't want to face that reality, so they run away in fear. And since they don't know which direction the storm is heading, they wind up running for a long time and get exhausted and even lost, until, when the storm eventually catches up with them, they wind up suffering through it for a long time. Whereas buffalo are wired to run into a storm—they embrace the suck, and as a result, they go straight through the storm to the other side. They get through it much faster, and as a result, their experience sucks less.

Whether your reality is a coming storm or a divorce or a balance sheet with a lot of red ink on it, you'll get through it in better shape if you act like the buffalo, or like Salem at boot camp, and embrace it instead of prolonging your agony and fighting it, like the cows. You don't have to do any more than that at this level. You don't have to work to try to change your situation. But you do have to accept the reality of it so you can move ahead. In fact, if you can't accept your reality, we've found that you're more likely to slide back down the mountain into waiting and hoping, or making excuses, or worse. We don't want that for you.

Now that you've acknowledged reality, now that you've seen what's in that 360-degree mirror that you were hiding from, you can't unsee it. We don't want you to turn around and go back to your past mindset, because the reality you acknowledged when you crossed the ravine moved you to being a victor. Going back would be lying to yourself about something you now clearly know. You would be denying reality, which will send you back to the other side of the ravine … back to victimhood.

And why would you want to do that?

It's not any better back there, on the other side of the ravine. So in order to stay on this side and remain a victor, you need to stick around to experience the pain of your reality. Because really experiencing your reality will, eventually, prepare you to deal with it. And once you do that, you can change it.

Remember, you can't do something about a problem until you acknowledge you have a problem. Living with and immersing yourself in that problem is what it means to truly own it. Embracing the suck means you will understand backward and forward those places where you are dissatisfied with your life. You'll know why you're there and what that entails. So you can finally make an informed decision as to what you want to do about it.

And sometimes, the answer to that question is nothing. There's a funny thing about embracing the suck. It can be terrifying—like it was terrifying for Robert to let go and sell his house. However, once you embrace the suck and fully accept your reality, once you own it, you may realize that it doesn't suck as much as you expected. Maybe it doesn't really suck at all. Or maybe, in your mind, your reality sucks less than the work it would take to change it. In those cases, staying where you are can be the right choice, as long as you make that choice with awareness and intent.

Remember, we don't always solve every dilemma, and that's okay. Just because you choose not to look for a solution to an issue right now doesn't mean you're ruling it out for later. Once you embrace the suck of any given situation, you get to do whatever you want about that situation as long as you leave your victim mentality behind. You can decide to stop where you are, or, if you're ready to start solving some of your problems and raising your satisfaction levels, you can continue to make your way up the mountain.

*Once you embrace the suck and fully accept your reality, once you own it, you may realize that it doesn't suck as much as you expected. Maybe it doesn't really suck at all.*

As we said before, that's going to involve some work. But it's work that brings great rewards.

# The Opportunity in the Suck

When you first acknowledged the reality of your situation, you were seeing it for the first time. When you embrace the suck, you take the time to fully examine your role in your reality. You see all sides of that reality, and when you do that, you see opportunities hiding right there in the suck that you didn't see before, because you weren't looking.

That might sound confusing, so let us try to make sense of it. When Salem didn't graduate high school, he acknowledged that he put himself in that position. He owned it. And he could have stopped there. After acknowledging the reality of "Well, I'm a high school dropout," he could have stayed there, living whatever the life of a high school dropout is supposed to be. After a while, he might have slipped back into blame or excuses or denial: "That stupid teacher ruined my life." Or "Hey, I'm a high school dropout, so I'm just going to kick back and party because nobody expects me to do jack."

For whatever reason, Salem wasn't wired that way, and seeing the empty chair next to Linh Tran and watching all his classmates graduate without him was more of a wake-up call. He decided to embrace the suck, which was "Holy shit, I'm a high school dropout. I'm going to have to work my ass off at a bunch of crappy jobs if I ever want to get anywhere in life." So that's what he did. While on one hand being stuck with the label of high school dropout sucked, it freed Salem to create his own path. And maybe that path was harder than the college-to-career pipeline, but it also gave him the opportunity to define himself and success on his own terms.

Acknowledging reality, looking in that mirror, and seeing all the places where you haven't measured up, where you aren't where or what you want to be, feels like a loss. And when you experience loss, you go through a grieving process. "Oh my God, the reason that I'm like this is my mother was an alcoholic, and I saw this growing up, and that's why I have these abusive relationships," or "Oh crap, I can't afford my lifestyle and I have to sell my house and all my stuff."

But as sad as your reality might be, there's opportunity there, even if you can't see it. Once you admit "This is who I am. This is what I do," you can actually follow up with "I need to do something different if my reality is going to change." Embracing the suck may sound like a downer, but it's actually empowering—because it takes you out of victimhood and puts you in a position to take control.

Not only is there a lot of power in simply accepting yourself, *not* accepting yourself can actually hurt you. According to Harvard Medical School's *Harvard Health Blog*, feeling negatively about yourself affects your brain in negative ways. Specifically, "the brain regions that help you control emotions and stress have less gray matter than someone with a greater degree of self-acceptance—that is, these regions actually have less tissue to 'work with.' This lack of gray matter may also appear in regions of the brain stem that process stress and anxiety." The stress signals from the brain stem also disrupt your emotional control regions.[14] Not accepting yourself puts all kinds of extra pressure on your brain, which makes everything even harder. It's a vicious cycle.

> *Embracing the suck may sound like a downer, but it's actually empowering—because it takes you out of victimhood and puts you in a position to take control.*

---

14    Srini Pillay, MD, "Greater Self-acceptance Improves Emotional Well-being," *Harvard Health Publishing*, May 16, 2016, https://www.health.harvard.edu/blog/greater-self-acceptance-improves-emotional-well-201605169546.

So, what does accepting yourself and your reality actually look like? Let's use the analogy of weight, since it's something most of us are familiar with. Once you've looked in the 360-degree mirror and acknowledged that you're twenty pounds overweight, what does it mean to go beyond acknowledgment and *embrace* it? It means you stop hiding your body in baggy clothes or packing it into Spanx or some sort of men's girdle or trying to squeeze into clothes that are too small to wear comfortably (or safely). You buy clothing in your actual size, not the size you wish you were, or a size that's so big you can't tell what size you are under all that fabric. You exist in the body you have, and you don't hide it or make excuses for it. And you stop thinking about the twenty extra pounds on your body and focus your energy on things you want to deal with.

We're not saying any of this is easy. That's why we use the word *suck* instead of *embrace the adventure!* or *embrace the fun!* Embracing reality is a lot of things, but fun is generally not one of them.

However, that doesn't mean it's not worth doing.

## Let's Make a Sucky Deal

One reason it can be hard to embrace the suck is that your brain isn't going to like it. Embracing the suck involves work, or at least the threat of work, and your brain would rather do almost anything than work. That's how we're all wired. Your brain is going to look for the easy way out, and in this case, instead of letting you own it, it's going to try to bargain. It's going to want to make a deal with the suck.

It works like this. Imagine if, after making the commitment to sell his house, Robert sold a bunch of furniture, and suddenly, since he had some money and could pay some of his bills, he started thinking, *Do we really need to sell the house? Now that we've downscaled our furniture …*

That's bargaining. You can acknowledge reality—*I'm broke,* or *I'm overweight,* or *I'm divorced*—but as soon as the work part comes in, your brain tries to take you back where it's safe. It says, "Maybe we don't have to go all the way to reality. Maybe we can take a few steps back." So you think, *Maybe I can just find a part-time job, and that will keep things afloat for a while longer, and I'll keep waiting . . .*

Backing out of a decision to acknowledge reality automatically pushes you back down the mountain. Once you've turned your back on that 360-degree mirror, it's easy to forget what you saw and shift your focus back to *My stupid boss cost me my job,* or *My parents never loved me,* or any of the filters or excuses you relied on to explain your reality before. Of course, all of those filters are just victim thinking. And they can drag you down really fast.

Embracing the suck means knowing it's going to hurt and committing to do it anyway. It means getting rid of furniture that you love. It means removing people from your life because they're toxic. It means saying goodbye to things that you found valuable because those things will lead you back down into victimization, where you were before. The only way not to get dragged back down is to embrace the suck, live it, and let it soak into you. Accept that this is your reality—it's your present and your immediate future, and it's going to be hard.

When you do that, something amazing happens. It gets a whole lot easier. When you embrace the suck, like those buffalo in the storm, you get through it. And on the other side, things look a whole lot better.

## The Other Side of the Suck

It's scary when, unlike boot camp or a rainstorm, you don't know what's on the other side of your suck, or even if there is another side.

Maybe you feel like your pain will never end, like this journey will last forever and you'll never feel better. What if you never get over that failed relationship, or the job you lost, or having to sell those home-theater chairs that recline? What if you have to feel like crap forever?

That's why people turn back. Like Robert did the first few times he dared to look at his bank statements. He saw the numbers, he did the math, but instead of embracing the suck, he did what most of us do. He did everything he could to wiggle around the suck. He refinanced his credit cards. He took out a loan against his house, which was basically like rearranging the deck chairs on the *Titanic*. But that's the perfect analogy for what happens when you acknowledge reality but don't fully embrace the suck. You slip right back into waiting and hoping ... and nothing gets better.

Until the pain of staying where you are is greater than the pain of what it takes to change. That's when you change.

Change starts when you stop running from the pain of where you are. That pain is your reality. It's the full truth. When you stop looking back for a reason or an excuse or a filter to tell you why it's not the truth, that's when the pain finally sinks in past all your barriers and you feel it. Again, it's like surrendering to the thing you've been fighting. Instead of immediately looking away or retreating or putting up a new filter, you keep looking in that mirror. You stay in the reality you acknowledged, almost soaking in it, saying, "This is my reality. Here I am. I need to find a way to get out of this. I don't know exactly where I'm going ... but I know I'm not going to go back to where I was."

And right there, where you understand that as bad as it is where you are, you know you don't want to go back ever again, you can find peace and a commitment to making the change.

Even though the suck sucks, there's a certain amount of peace in saying, "I finally accepted reality. I finally embraced it. I'm no longer telling myself lies, and I'm not going backward." You let your brain process it instead of spending all your energy fighting it, which means you can finally deal with it. This may not reduce the actual suck level, but we do know it teaches you the discipline of not being a victim. You move from a place where everything's crappy and everything's dumping all over you to "Hey, life is hard, but I'm kicking its butt. I'm making a change. I'm intentionally moving in a direction to get better."

That's what happened when Robert and Kathy moved into the rental house. The first few times they woke up and didn't have all the things that they'd had in their old house, they felt disoriented and depressed. Then there were the dumb little issues that always pop up in a new place, like the fact that there was no vent for the stove, so whenever they cooked, the house filled with smoke until the alarm went off.

That sucked.

But then again …

After Robert and Kathy got the money from the house sale, Robert contacted the federal government to pay his back taxes. He contacted all his credit card companies and paid them all off too. And then one morning, Robert woke up and thought, *Oh my gosh—this is what peace feels like.*

He had forgotten what it was like to not have anxiety, because he'd lived with it for so long it had become his normal existence.

When you stop holding on to what doesn't serve you and embrace the suck, you can also find that peace.

So let's do it.

# ACCOUNTABILITY EXERCISE: SURVIVING THE SUCK

Whatever you've been through in your life, whatever your reality is right now, we have one big piece of good news for you.

You're still here.

Whatever you've been through, as much as it might have sucked, you have a 100 percent positive record of surviving it. And that's actually pretty awesome. You're a survivor, and you didn't even know it. So today we're going to build on that success and grow your confidence for the rest of our journey by reminding you of just how much you've already accomplished.

Think back on all the things in your life that happened that really sucked. Remember that time when you were a kid and you failed a test or didn't make the team? Write it down. Your first breakup? Write it down. A bad decision that really cost you? Absolutely write that down. Losing a job, a home, a business? Write those down too.

As bad as all of those things were, guess what? You're still here. You survived them. You *won.*

Now, think about each of those things you've written down and *how* you survived them. Maybe you didn't do much at all, and it was just a matter of time passing. Or maybe you buckled down and did a lot of work. Whatever you did, even if it was nothing, write that down too.

When you've finished, you'll have a tangible reminder that you can embrace the suck and survive, including some techniques that have worked for you in the past and maybe a few that, at the time, didn't work quite as well. But those don't matter, because right there in front of you is a list of things you've overcome, even when the overcoming was ugly.

You did it all those times before. You can do it again!

You can do more than you ever imagined you could. And now that you've embraced the suck, you are ready to create a plan and move onward. In the next chapter we'll begin that final push toward the top of the mountain. Are you excited? We are!

# CHAPTER NINE

## The Final Ascent

*Start where you are. Use what you have. Do what you can.*

—**ARTHUR ASHE**

When Robert and Kathy embraced the suck and sold their house, a funny thing happened.

Their lives got better. Almost instantly.

It helped that, when they embraced reality, they chose to commit to their new life. They could have gritted their teeth and said, "Our life sucks. We have to live in this crappy rental house, so we're going to be pissed and disgruntled the whole time." They could have been victims. A lot of people would have reacted that way. But Robert and Kathy chose not to be. That doesn't mean they wanted to sell their house and all their stuff. It just meant they were moving forward, which meant focusing on what was in front of them, not behind them. Their old life in their old house was behind them. So they made a promise to each other. "Let's make the best of this. Let's never complain. Let's figure out how to see everything positively."

There was a lot to be positive about. Instead of winding up in some awful hovel, they found a really nice rental home that had just been remodeled that also happened to be really convenient to their son James's school. Robert felt like God had provided them with that house when they took that step away from victimhood. The landlords were so gracious, they said Robert and Kathy could change anything they wanted about the house, and they, the landlords, would pay for it. So Robert and his son James did lots of improvements outside and in, and even installed a vent over the stove so the house wouldn't get smoky when they cooked. Not all landlords are willing to pay for remodeling a house that is already rented, so they were very grateful.

Piece by piece, as their new home became more comfortable, so did Robert and Kathy. Saying goodbye to their dream house was hard and painful, but when they did it, they turned a corner. For the first time in a long time, things were getting better instead of worse. And Robert began to see his life (and the world) differently.

For years, Robert's life had been defined by stress. "How will I pay this bill? How can I get more clients? What can I do to stop the bleeding?" Now, suddenly, poof! The stress was gone. In its place was a kind of peace Robert hadn't felt in years. Every morning, instead of waking up in a panic, he woke up smiling. It felt so good to know he didn't need anything from anybody that he acquired a kind of swagger. He'd go to meetings, and instead of bending over backward to convince a prospective client to sign on the dotted line, he'd say, "Hey, this is what I do. Do you think this is something you'd want to do? No? Okay. Goodbye." He could move on without anxiety, without feeling like he couldn't afford to lose this client, because he actually could.

All because Robert embraced his reality and accepted account-ability for his debt. In other words, he finally owned it.

As soon as he did, he started finding solutions.

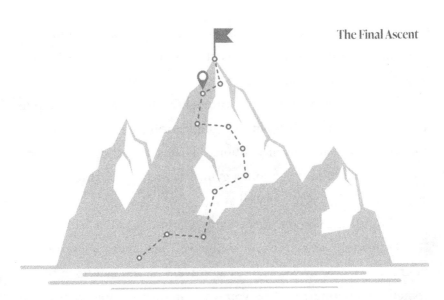

# You Are Here

Once you stop fighting reality and embrace it—once you own the things you're not satisfied with in your life and accept them as reality—you can finally deal with that reality. Solutions start to appear, almost by magic, where you felt powerless and helpless. It's like you've removed a physical barrier that stands between you and satisfaction.

You can't get clarity about how much something bothers you and affects your life until you accept and embrace it. Once you let yourself feel, acknowledge, and experience your reality, you may see that reality in a different way. You will see problems that you want to solve, and you will also discover areas where something you were 100 percent certain sucked isn't actually all that bad. You get to make that choice. Sometimes, like with Robert's debt, the problem demands solving as soon as you know it's there. But at other times, you may only see something as a problem because other people do, or because you think other people do. As long as something is not standing between you and satisfaction, it's not really a problem.

Let's go back, once again, to those twenty extra pounds. When you embrace the reality that you're twenty pounds overweight, suddenly you have a lot of options. Seeing those twenty pounds as what they really are—pounds—instead of through a filter that adds emotion to the equation reduces them to a simple problem to solve. And that can trigger an avalanche of solutions. "I can stop getting takeout and cook healthier food. I can join a gym. I can read a nutrition book. I can get a health coach." As well as …

"I don't care about losing twenty pounds. I can live with it."

Ultimately, what matters is how you feel about those twenty pounds, or whatever you view as a problem. If you can honestly say something no longer bothers you, you can do absolutely nothing to change it and still be a victor, not a victim.

Nobody summits every mountain. There might be extenuating circumstances. It may actually be too hard. Or, once you embrace the reality of a situation, what you saw as a mountain might look more like a molehill. Can you imagine how freeing that is? When something you thought was a problem no longer weighs on you or makes you unhappy, you can move on to other things. Because, at this point, there are probably more important mountains you want to climb.

# Moving Up

One way to decide where you want to keep climbing and where it's okay to stop is to revisit your Satisfaction Wheels. When you accept your reality, the numbers on those wheels might look different. Maybe, in some areas, your satisfaction levels have changed as you've climbed out of the muck and become more accountable. Or maybe when you look at them again, you'll realize some of your numbers were off in the first place. Something you marked as a four may feel more like an eight when you think about it now. While at the same time, something you gave a high number, where you thought you were doing just fine, may suddenly bother you now that you're owning more aspects of your life.

This is all normal and an important part of this step. You're not going to solve every problem, you're not going to change everything in your life, especially not the moment you accept that those problems are there. But once you open the door to reality, you can start to prioritize. Whether you decide to move forward or to be content where you're at, you're no longer a victim because you've taken control and made the choice to live according to your own values.

As for those things you decide you want to change, when you embrace reality, solutions tend to come really fast. Almost too fast. Once that mental barrier that's been standing between you and satisfaction is gone, once you finally accept and embrace that you are who you are, the solutions almost erupt out of you. So you need to be discerning and weed out things that, when you think them through, don't make sense. To do that, it's helpful to make sure your goals are SMART goals.

If you're in business or have ever read a business book, chances are you've already heard of SMART goals. But they work in any context, not just business. That's because, while SMART doesn't refer to the fact that the goals themselves are smart (although they are), it's an acronym for the five things a goal absolutely needs to be if you hope to reach it. They are as follows:

1. **Specific**, meaning you define a specific thing you want to accomplish (*I want to lose twenty pounds, not lose "weight."*)

2. **Measurable**, meaning you can quantify and track your progress (*I want to lose twenty pounds, not "some weight."*)

3. **Achievable**, meaning you have or can acquire the capability to do this thing (*I will lose twenty pounds by changing my diet and adding regular exercise,* not *I will lose twenty pounds by drinking a magic potion every night.*)

4. **Realistic**, meaning this thing can actually be done (*I will lose twenty pounds by the end of eighteen months, not by the end of this month.*)

This is a big one for us. Our biggest disappointments tend to happen when we have unrealistic expectations.

And finally ...

5. **Timely**, meaning you commit to doing this thing by a specific day or time (*I will lose twenty pounds by the end of next year,* not *I will lose twenty pounds ... "someday."*)

When you're done, you should have a goal that looks something like this:

*I will lose twenty pounds by the end of next year by removing desserts from my diet and adding regular exercise three times a week for forty minutes.*

A good, workable solution that will move you forward should fit all five of those parameters. If your solution doesn't, it may not be viable, meaning it may be time to move on to your next idea and see if it's better. We'll get more into how to decide whether or not to pursue a specific solution a little later.

# But First ...

Before you get too excited about how you're going to change your entire life the minute you put this book down, we want to make sure something is clear. Yes, we're working on solutions; however, *reading this book isn't going to solve your problems for you!* Reading a book won't put a million dollars in your pocket or save your marriage, no matter how awesome that book may be. Our goal with this book is to give you the *tools* that will help you get those things if they're what you really, actually want.

That starts with defining what you want, as opposed to what you think you should want, or what other people want you to want. When you zero in on the things you want from life, and what you need to do to get there, that's when you start finding the solutions that will bring you closer to that reality.

And one more thing ... deciding to own it and stop being a victim is not going to automatically erase all the bad things in your life. When Salem woke up the morning after he tried to kill himself and decided he was going to do things differently, nothing else had changed. His wife didn't magically change her mind about taking the kids and moving away. He still had to walk that long road of divorce and alienation. Owning it didn't fix any of that.

What it did, and what was so powerful about it, was give him a place to start.

Once Salem acknowledged where he was, once he embraced the reality that his marriage was over and his soon-to-be-ex-wife and kids would be moving away and he was never going to be that person who lived that life ever again, he could finally move forward.

Sometimes, embracing the suck can be so painful that you go back and forth between thinking you've embraced reality and realizing you actually haven't. How many people, after a breakup, work on themselves for a hot minute, make a little bit of progress, and immediately announce, "I'm going to win them back!" We've all been there. But remember, when you turn your back on reality, on what you know to be true, you slide back down the mountain. So look at it this way.

If your solution is to go back to where you came from, even if you think you're "better," the mere fact that you're going backward pretty much guarantees it's not a solution. Or it's not a solution to the right problem. Part of owning it is reminding yourself of what the right problem is—of what reality is—until you've accepted it to the point where you no longer question it. It may seem like a simple thing, but there's huge value in simply accepting what is.

Also understand that every solution you pursue isn't necessarily going to be the right solution. Becoming accountable doesn't give you magic powers. When something doesn't work out the way you hope or expect it will—and it will—don't give up and go back to being a victim. Remember, it's supposed to be hard. That's why you embrace the suck. Ultimately, solving a problem may take time. It may take years. You may try multiple solutions before finding one that works. But as long as you have a plan, and you're sticking to that plan, you're going to get there.

# Making Your Plan

Once you have a goal in mind, the next step is to make a plan to make it happen. Having a plan is essential. It's the map that's going to guide you from your reality—where you are now—to where you want to be. And in order to make sure the plan is as smart as your goal, it should include all five aspects of a SMART goal. That means it should be a plan to do something specific, where the progress can be measured, that is both attainable and reasonable, and that can be done in a specific time frame. And in order to make sure you don't forget this carefully constructed and well-thought-out plan, we have four words for you:

*Put it in writing!*

A study by Dr. Gail Matthews, psychology professor at the Dominican University in California, revealed that you are 42 percent more likely to achieve your goals if you write them down.[15] Writing something down forces you to think it through logically while leaving you with a document you can refer back to again and again. That document then becomes a tool you can use to remind yourself of where you are in the process of getting where you want to go and see whether or not you're on track. You know, like a map.

Writing something down also has a psychological effect. It's a way of telling the world, "Here's what I'm going to do." It can be such a powerful tool that, after surviving his suicide attempt, Salem put it in writing on his body by getting a tattoo marking the moment his new life began. The tattoo may not say *This is my starting point*, but that's what it means to Salem. Every time he sees it (which is often, since it's on his arm), it reminds him that he'll never go back to being the person he was before that day.

## Share Your Plan

Once you've formulated a plan and put it in writing, the next step is to share that plan with someone else. This gives you another level of accountability … but not because you've enlisted another person to "hold you accountable." Unfortunately, in our experience, the idea of an "accountability partner" is BS. Calling someone your accountability partner doesn't give them the power to hold you accountable. They don't know when you're being honest and when you're hiding things. And while they may be able to see a different perspective on

---

15   Peter Economy, "This Is the Way You Need to Write Down Your Goals for Faster Success," *Inc.*, February 28, 2018, https://www.inc.com/peter-economy/this-is-way-you-need-to-write-down-your-goals-for-faster-success.html.

your plan that you don't, they can't make you see those issues or do anything about them.

No one can really hold you accountable except you.

However, other people can help you in your quest to be accountable if you're as honest with them about your reality as you are now being with yourself. In his book *Principles,* Ray Dalio outlines an approach he calls "radical transparency." It was sparked when, after reaching success in business, he lost everything because he wouldn't listen to what other people had to say. Once he realized this was the reason for his downfall, he made a commitment to let others into his world and be completely open minded about their comments and suggestions.

> *No one can really hold you accountable except you.*

Radical transparency involves getting other people to engage with you in what's called *thoughtful disagreement.* Instead of relying on your own interpretation of reality, you invite other people in specifically to question it and poke holes in it. Being willing to listen to others who see things in a different way gives you a more complete picture of your reality, including any blind spots, so you can test your solutions to make sure they're viable. It can feel uncomfortable at times, but it has the power to help you reach your goal.

The key to all of it is transparency. If you're not transparent enough to acknowledge a problem to other people, nobody can help you find a solution. And even then, simply acknowledging the problem isn't enough. You also need to remain open to other people's input, even if you hear things you don't want to hear. If you can withstand that and not shut down, you wind up with more, possibly better options. Allowing people who don't see the world through your filters to disagree with you can open your eyes toward other ways of looking at things and reveal solutions you might not have considered. And continuing to be radically transparent with those people gives you additional support in working toward your goals.

Robert and Kathy used this approach when they decided to get out of debt. Instead of relying on their own expertise and trusting themselves to stay on track, they hired a professional to help them set up and follow a budget. They paid him $200 a month to look at everything they were doing with their money and ask them questions about it. Was it fun to hear a near stranger ask, "Why are you spending so much on that? Do you really want this?" on a regular basis? Of course not! It was like putting their finances in front of a 360-degree mirror and revealing all of their flaws, for six long months. But this near stranger knew things they didn't know and could see things they couldn't see, and he helped them break some really bad habits. He helped them get where they wanted to go—but only because they were willing to be radically transparent and vulnerable.

*Allowing people who don't see the world through your filters to disagree with you can open your eyes toward other ways of looking at things and reveal solutions you might not have considered.*

The truth is, if you want to be better, you need other people around you. That's the core premise of Robert's business, but this isn't a business book, and getting you to join one of Robert's groups is not our purpose here. Our purpose is to help you make your life better, and we both know that having the right people around—people who can encourage you and celebrate the victories along the way, and also help you stay focused and committed to the process—can certainly do that.

# When Salem Met Robert

Robert's CEO groups are all about constantly learning how to be a better version of yourself. The monthly group meetings provide an environment for people to get fresh ideas and support we all need in our journey. His clients are committed to being radically transparent, radically open minded, and engaged in thoughtful disagreement in their pursuit of the life and business they really want. (Visit www. REFdallas.com for more information about Robert's groups.)

All of this really appealed to Salem. As a CEO, he had a lot of responsibilities, and as a natural contrarian, he wanted people who would kick his butt or offer a hug as needed to support him in his journey to be his best. The idea of being in a room where he could get that from eleven other CEOs sounded like the exact thing he needed. So he joined the group.

Around this time, Salem was butting heads with his family about how the business should be run. While he was on vacation in Cabo, one conversation was so bad that Salem left the beach to call Robert and vent. He told Robert he was so tired of the family drama he was ready to leave his own company and go work somewhere else.

At first, Robert just listened. He wasn't emotionally involved, so he could clearly see what Salem couldn't: first, that exasperating as it was, the situation was manageable, and second and more importantly, that it didn't need to be managed in the middle of Salem's vacation! He was able to talk Salem down and convince him to enjoy the rest of his time off and deal with business when he got home. And it worked. Seeing his situation through someone else's eyes enabled Salem to calm down, enjoy his trip, and come up with a solution that worked for him.

People aren't always comfortable sharing their problems because, let's face it, it can be embarrassing. Robert has seen this with some clients who didn't allow themselves to be accountable in life. Not long after he started his company, he had a client who was very bright and talented but was making a lot of really bad decisions. This client was a new business owner and would share the real challenges the company was facing in private conversations with Robert. But in group sessions, this new business owner would never talk about what was really going on. Radical transparency isn't always easy, but it has great rewards. This client's lack of transparency meant they were deprived of the collective wisdom of the others in the group, most of whom had started multiple businesses and could have offered insights that would have helped. Instead, the business almost went bankrupt.

Robert understands that standing in front of a group and saying, "I made this stupid mistake—what should I do?" might sound like torture. But if this person had brought their problems to the group, no one would have judged them as weak. Instead, they would have helped them create a plan, measured progress monthly, and cheered them along the way to success.

But they couldn't, because they weren't invited in.

Everyone has blind spots. That's where someone who has been down the same road but isn't looking at it with the emotion that you have attached to it can really help. It also helps to get the perspective of someone who has already done the thing you're trying to do. You don't go to your cousin Todd, who doesn't ever seem to be able to pay his rent, and say, "How should I get out of debt?" You go to the guy who owns a business, who's rocked it, who knows what he's doing. If you're trying to save your marriage, you go to someone who's got a good marriage—you don't drown your sorrows with your buddy whose wife just left him. If you're trying to lose weight, you ask someone who's healthy. That's one of the reasons the peer groups Robert leads are so powerful. With twelve people in a room, there's almost no situation you could possibly go through that someone hasn't already experienced. So instead of having to find solutions on your own, you have input from qualified people who can share their own experiences. They can offer knowledge you would never have without them.

Sometimes, people will even offer resources, like we do in our group. We've had members say, "Hey, let me send over one of my employees—they're really good in this area." Or "Let me introduce you to my banker. They have a solution for that." Or even "Let me help you here." There's so much help available when it comes to finding solutions—you just need to be smart enough to know where to look … and brave enough to ask.

We understand that you might not have access to a CEO group like Robert's, or might not have a need for one. However, we all have family, friends, and other groups in our personal and professional lives where we can get support. Just be sure to choose the people you turn to during this process wisely.

## Living in Your New Reality

While we're on the subject of other people, we need to point out that unfortunately not everyone you know and care about is going to help you find solutions. In fact, they may be part of the problem. When you're climbing the Accountability Mountain, some people who are part of your world are going to hold you back. At other times, your environment itself can hold you back. That means that if you're going to stop being a victim and live a victorious life, you will have to say goodbye to people, places, and things that were part of your life when you were a victim.

One of Salem's friends, who moved to Texas from the ghettos of Boston, put it this way: "I wanted a different life for myself than I was being given." Salem was in the same situation when he started his new life after his wife left him. He wasn't just divorcing his wife—he had to divorce his friends and his old life in order to live in his new reality and not slide back into the old one. It was hard and it was painful, but at the same time, Salem knew that if he was around those people, his solutions would be eroded. He had embraced a new reality, but those people had not, which meant that they would drag him back down the mountain.

Many of the It's Too Hard people and the Wait and Hope people, the people that supported your excuses and blame, or thought you tried hard enough, may not support you as you climb the Accountability Mountain. They might seem supportive. They might say things like, "Oh my gosh, you're doing so great. I'm so proud of you." But often the people who were part of your problems ultimately can't be part of your solutions. Instead, they are often the saboteurs as you pursue a better version of your life.

This doesn't mean everyone in your "old life" is a bad person. You had a role to play in the way your relationships developed. You probably neglected to tell the people closest to you that you were making excuses, or blaming others, or waiting and hoping for your life to change. They might have supported your choices because they only knew the parts of the story you let them know. Or maybe they failed to speak truth in your life because they did not want to rock the boat. Or calling you out would be like the pot calling the kettle black, because they have their own issues with accountability and victim behavior.

In other words, you don't have to kick everyone you know out of your life. However, you do need to let the people you remain involved with know that you're a different person, you're doing things differently, to expect different things from you—and that you will be asking for their support on this journey. Just be sure to do it with humility. If you go around bragging about how awesome you are now that you got your act together and talk down to other people, you're setting yourself up to fail the first time you hit the wall. And you will. You need to stay humble about this process—there will be ups and downs, and the minute you feel like you have all the answers, you'll learn how wrong you were.

## Avoiding Potential Pitfalls

Chances are you'll learn that lesson multiple times. The mere fact that you are making better choices this year than you did last year can be very disarming. Just taking steps toward satisfaction and getting closer to achieving your goal feels good. You're taking action! You're making things happen! Which means you can easily be lulled into feeling like, *Hey, I'm doing okay* and take your eyes off the prize before you reach the goal you set.

That's why everything we talked about earlier in this chapter— choosing SMART goals, putting them in writing, involving other people, and measuring your progress—is so important. Together, those things will tell you if your plan is working and, if it isn't, help you make a change. You're going to need that kind of support as you make your way up this mountain. There will be times where you feel like you're in a ditch and nothing is going right. Having metrics and measuring your progress every week or quarter or whatever makes sense will help you spot problems early so you can make adjustments and stay on track. It also helps you see that you are actually making progress when you feel like it's taking too long.

Another good reason to surround yourself with people who have wisdom but are not burdened with the same emotions you have about your challenges is that they can speak truth into your life when you get stuck. This can be a long journey, and you will be tempted to stop along the way. You will get tired. It's still hard. When the air's thin and the weather's blowing at you, if you're all alone, who's even going to know if you turn back? If you're being radically transparent with someone, and you say, "Look, I'm thinking about stopping," they'll know. They'll be able to say, "Okay, tell me how that's going to work in your situation. Is that going to align with your goals?" They can talk you out of sabotaging yourself. Whereas if it's just you, you can talk yourself into whatever you want to do with warm fuzzy thoughts of how well it's all going to work out. And when it doesn't, and you fail because you deviated from the plan, and you feel like you're a loser, you quit. Then you start sliding down the mountain, and you wind up right back in some other place you don't want to be.

That's why now is the time to surround yourself with people of excellence in your own life. You may have heard that you're the sum of the five people you spend the most time with. If you want to be a quality person, those five people who are closest to you need to be quality people too. Whether you need someone to kick your butt or someone to give you a hug, or both, look for people you can count on to do it in a way that continues to push you toward getting better.

Again, those people aren't going to solve your problems, and neither are we. Remember, *nobody cares* about your problems. Solving them is not their job, and it's also not our job. Our job is to show you that you can come up with your own solutions. Surround yourself with great people, do your homework, read a book, watch a video, and find your solution. Just know that whatever your problems are, they can be solved. It might take time and it might be painful, but when you compare it to being a victim, it's still a better way to live.

And when you get there, it's like coming over the mountain and looking over a beautiful valley.

---

*Surround yourself with great people, do your homework, read a book, watch a video, and find your solution. Just know that whatever your problems are, they can be solved.*

The journey has been long and hard until now. You could stop here, but you'd be stopping where it's coldest and the weather is harsh. So stick with us. Take a deep breath, enjoy the view for a little bit, and then put your head down and do the work. You are almost home!

## ACCOUNTABILITY EXERCISE: MAKE YOUR PLAN

Now that you have acknowledged reality and embraced the suck, we're going to put everything you've learned into practice and start finding your own solutions.

1. Choose just ONE area where you're not satisfied.

2. What is your current reality? What is the situation you want to address? Write it here.

3. What do you want to do to change this situation to be satisfied?

4. Write your solution in the form of a SMART goal:

   **Specific**

   **Measurable**

**Attainable**

**Realistic**

**Timely**

Now that your goal is clear, determine the steps you need to take to achieve your SMART goal. Make sure you list as many details as you can of the steps, in order with numbers, to track progress in a time frame that is realistic and attainable.

**Step 1**

**Step 2**

**Step 3**

Keep writing as long as you need space to create a clear plan that you're excited about.

1. Share your plan with a wise friend who has agreed to be radically transparent with you. Ask them what else you might consider in this effort and where they see what could be blind spots in the plan. Invite them to follow up and support you in your journey.

2. Set a date to share your progress with this friend and measure your results, during which you will give them an update and be radically open to their questions (and potential disagreements).

3. Adjust your efforts as needed to stay on course, and agree to meet again to update the process.

Lastly, share your journey with us. Email us at Info@ NobodyCaresBook.com so we can see your plans and celebrate your victories along the way.

# CHAPTER TEN

## Reaching the Summit

*There will be obstacles. There will be doubters. There will be mistakes. But with hard work, there are no limits.*

—**MICHAEL PHELPS**

When Robert and Kathy sold their house, they didn't have any expectations beyond paying off their debts and putting an end to their financial stress. They didn't think anything else would change, let alone get better, and that was not the reason they decided to sell. They had reached the point where they realized the pain of selling their house could not possibly be worse than the pain they were already experiencing.

They had faced their reality, and part of that reality was that Robert's business was not generating enough money to sustain their lifestyle. After five years of trying everything he knew to build a successful coaching and peer-learning business, his entire clientele consisted of just one group of nine people. He couldn't help wondering if maybe God was trying to send him a message. Every time he added someone to the group, someone else would leave. Or he'd add two members and lose one, but then, a few months later, he'd add one and lose two. It was this constant cycle of up and down, up and down, but never up high enough to fill even one group to capacity, let alone start another one. Robert started to wonder: *Maybe he's telling me he's only going to provide just enough, and I need to be content with that.*

If that was the case, if that was what God wanted, then there really wasn't a question. Robert needed to adjust his lifestyle so he could be content with what God was giving him. And he had been given a lot. He had a loving marriage to a beautiful wife. He had two wonderful children. He had his salvation and a personal relationship with Jesus Christ. So Robert and Kathy made the choice to stop being victims, face reality, and sell their house, because it was the right thing to do. The only thing they expected in return was peace of mind.

But they got so much more.

Once Robert cleared away all the head trash that comes with being a victim, he felt different. His focus was clearer, especially since he no longer needed to do things out of desperation or panic or fear. If a would-be client didn't sign up for coaching or join the group, so what? He didn't need that client. If he had to, he could take a job at Walmart and still take care of his family and pay the bills.

That same swagger started to seep into his coaching relationships with his existing clients. He started challenging them in ways he hadn't before, pushing them to be more transparent and providing more thoughtful disagreement when it was warranted. After all, if he wasn't going to tell them the truth, even when it hurt, what kind of coach would that make him? If he lost opportunities and clients because they didn't welcome his radical transparency, that was fine with him.

But a funny thing happened. Robert didn't lose clients. He gained clients. A lot of them!

And because they were clear about what Robert was offering and what they needed to do to get the most out of his CEO groups, those groups got stronger. As of this writing, his business has tripled. All because Robert did the thing he said he was going to do. He executed his plan, and by doing that, he reached the top of the mountain.

He made it to the summit.

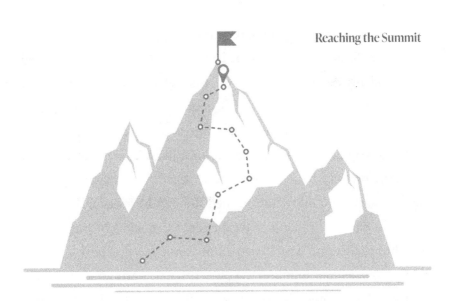

# You Are Here

You don't need us to tell you when you've reached the summit of the Accountability Mountain. You'll know it in your soul, because as long as it's taken to get here, reaching the top is actually the simplest, most basic thing in the world.

You reach the top when you do exactly what you say you're going to do.

That's it.

There's a reason "Just Do It" has been Nike's tagline since 1987. It's so simple, but at the same time, it's the secret to everything. Because until you do whatever the specific thing is you need to do, whatever problem you're dealing with, until you do what you said you're going to do about it, you have no idea how the story ends. Until you execute your plan, you don't know what's going to happen. Even if you expect that your life will change, there's no way to know exactly how.

> *You reach the top when you do exactly what you say you're going to do. That's it.*

That's the moment where the magic happens.

When Robert sold his house, he had a goal in mind. He planned to pay off his debts and start over, and he achieved that goal. But reaching that peak was only the beginning of the good things that happened when Robert finally became accountable. That one act started a trophic cascade of good things, just like the wolves when they were brought back to Yellowstone. Instead of simply paying off his debts, accountability transformed Robert's business and his life.

You may not immediately experience that kind of transformation, but there's one sure way to tell if you've reached peak accountability. Look at your numbers. If you've been measuring your progress, your numbers should give you all the information you need to know that you've reached your goal. If your reality matches whatever you wrote down when you put your goal in writing, if you did the thing you said you would do, that means you've made it. Numbers don't lie.

The number on your Satisfaction Wheel should back up the fact that you've reached your goal. If they don't show that you're happier and more satisfied in whatever area you've been working on, that could mean there's a disconnect, but don't panic. The goal you defined might not have been the right goal, or there may be more work to do to get there than you anticipated when you wrote your plan. But even if you hit a dead end, as long as you have the experience of doing what you were going to do, you're halfway there. When you go back and look at what went wrong, you can make a better plan and do it again. Regardless, the mere fact that you made a plan and followed through means that you have reached the summit and are living life as a victor!

So … cue the fireworks and strike up the band. Congratulations! You're finally victorious.

# Now What?

Once you make it to the top of the mountain, you might start to experience things you didn't expect that had nothing to do with your initial goal. When you're not a victim, you're no longer bogged down with the baggage of filters and excuses and blame and feeling not good enough and waiting and hoping or any of that head trash. You're not as concerned about what everybody else is thinking or little inconveniences like traffic or disagreements with other people that might have derailed you before. You don't whine or complain. Instead, you radiate clarity and confidence, and because of that, people want to be associated with you and be a part of your world.

This happens because your accountability demonstrates to other people that you're someone they can trust. When you do what you say you're going to, you're being true to yourself, and when you're true to yourself, people trust that you will be true to them as well. It's almost like a light that emanates from you, that you're finally living your purpose in life or doing what you're supposed to do. Other people are drawn in by that light and care enough to help you. You become like a magnet, attracting what you need to achieve your goals in the future.

If that sounds like the most amazing thing in the world, we're not gonna lie—it is. But remember, we're talking about life in reality. So it's not going to be all rainbows and unicorns. It's even going to suck sometimes. Trust us on that one. But when you own it, when you just keep going

> *When you do what you say you're going to, you're being true to yourself, and when you're true to yourself, people trust that you will be true to them as well.*

and keep doing what you said you were going to do (and of course making adjustments when necessary because you're not an idiot), you get through the suck a lot faster. Sometimes you can even avoid it.

The trap that people tend to fall into at this stage—yes, there is one, even on top of the mountain—is being focused on the goal and not the journey. After all, if you're only focused on the goal, when you reach the top of the mountain, the journey's pretty much over, right? But this process is never over, because there are always new mountains to climb. That's what makes this a journey and makes what we've been doing here a journey-focused process as opposed to a goal-focused process.

Which means ... what, exactly? Say you were dissatisfied with your financial situation, and you set a goal of becoming a millionaire. Making that million dollars would be a goal-focused process, because it would be all about hitting that number. A journey-focused process is about how each step you take and each little change you make alters your level of satisfaction. You might discover you don't need a million dollars to be satisfied. And you might decide to pursue something other than a million dollars once you make that discovery.

That's what we've been doing here. We didn't write this book to deliver you a million dollars, although if it does, and that's what you want, great. But this is about more than that. We're here to deliver *satisfaction*. Dare we even say *happiness*?

So how do you know if you've really reached the top of the mountain? Think about the journey you've been on and where you are right now, and ask yourself, "Am I satisfied?" Not "Am I richer?" or "Do I have a better job?" or "Am I thinner?" but "Am I content with where I am today? Am I truly happy?" Because when you clear away all the head trash, which includes other people's expectations of what satisfaction should look like, how you *feel,* your actual level of satisfaction and happiness, is all that really matters.

This is important, because you can actually make that million dollars, or get that promotion, or lose those twenty pounds and discover that you're not happier. Achieving goals isn't what makes you a victor. You stopped being a victim—you stopped ignoring and blaming and making excuses and giving up and waiting and hoping. You accepted and embraced your reality, and you found solutions to change what about your reality you decided needed changing. That is what made you a victor in life, and *that* enabled you to achieve those goals. When you become a victor, you finally get to lead your life instead of letting your life lead you.

When you experience that feeling, even if you realize you're not exactly where you want to be, your brain gets it and feels rewarded. And you set new goals, and the journey continues.

# Staying on Top

Continuing the journey up the mountain, to new peaks of accountability, is just a matter of developing a habit of doing what you say you're going to do. You can develop a good habit as easily as you develop a bad one—you just have to be intentional about it for a period of time, until it becomes second nature. As Mel Robbins says, "You are not a procrastinator; you developed a *habit* of procrastination." In order to stay at the top of the mountain, you have to develop a habit of doing what you said you were going to do, without negotiation, excuses, or compromise. Stick to the plan, do those things, see where they take you, then evaluate later, when you reach a milestone or when you're done.

That's the only way you can ever really know what the outcome will be. Like Nike, you just do it.

Once you do, once you've done it and you've reached that summit, it's a lot easier to do the next thing, and the next thing, and the next thing. It's like a muscle you develop that gets stronger and stronger. Not that you need to do that next thing right away. Don't immediately start beating up on yourself, thinking, *Oh no, I still haven't done this and this!* Take a break and bask in your success and how much you achieved. Let yourself feel good for a change. Even if you don't actually ever reach this summit, as long as you operate at a high level of accountability to yourself, you deserve to celebrate where you are, up above the muck, high on a beautiful mountain.

And then again, if you do reach that summit, it's never the end of the journey. What would happen if you stayed on top of Everest? You'd die. And honestly, if you're content with where you're at forever, having conquered just one problem, and that's all that matters, that is a kind of death, and the rest of your life will suck. So remember, reaching the summit is an important thing, but it's not everything. There's a whole rest of your life that you need to maintain and grow and live. But as you do, and you're faced with those challenges, you'll meet them knowing you don't have to be a victim anymore. You have been fully accountable, and now you know what that feels like moving forward. And it gets easier the next time and the next time and the next time, because you've learned that the things that are scary are never as scary as you think.

 ## ACCOUNTABILITY EXERCISE: CELEBRATE JUST DOING IT

You've reached the top of the mountain before, maybe without even knowing it. Which means you may not have acknowledged or celebrated it. So that's what we're going to do now.

We want you to take a minute to think through some of the accomplishments you've achieved so far, just to get you started thinking about the journey ahead. And because it's about the journey starting now, we want you to start your list with the fact that you bought and read this book—that's an accomplishment on its own. Think about other things you've done that some people in this world never get to attempt. We'll make a few assumptions about you to get you started:

1. Bought and read *Nobody Cares*

2. Went to school (yes, many people never get to do that!)

3. Graduated high school

4. Raised two kids

5.

6.

7.

8.

9.

10.

11.

Even though they might look like simple things, does this list help you see how much you've already accomplished? Now you are ready to do even more.

That's all there is to it. Do what you say you're going to do. That's what peak accountability looks like.

In the next chapter, we'll look at what happens when you lose your grip on accountability and slip and fall back down the mountain. Because yes, it's going to happen.

# CHAPTER ELEVEN

## Falling Down

*Success consists of going from failure to failure without loss of enthusiasm.*

−**WINSTON CHURCHILL**

Once they got settled in their new house, Robert and Kathy's new life started taking shape. One of the first things they did was walk around their neighborhood and introduce themselves to all their neighbors. They never did that in the old neighborhood—and soon they had more friends in their new community than they had made in six years in the old one. They adjusted to living in a smaller house and used the money they made selling their old furniture to buy furniture that would work in their new cozier space. Of course, the house was a rental, so there was only so much they could do to put their personal stamp on it. But they did everything within the realm of possibility to make it feel like home, and it did. It was all coming together ...

And then the holidays came.

Now normally, the holidays were a very special time for Kathy and Robert because it meant extra time with family and friends. Kathy spent weeks preparing and decorating and days in the kitchen cooking and baking so they were ready for guests. From late November through New Year's, the house was packed with people eating and laughing and watching movies upstairs in the movie theater and building memories around the giant Christmas tree. It was something Kathy looked forward to each year.

But that year was going to be different.

Because there wasn't enough space in the new house to put everyone.

Robert and Kathy typically hosted about twenty people at the holidays—that's what that massive dining room table with the twenty chairs was for. The absolute most they could fit in their new place was ten, and even that would be a squeeze. Which meant Kathy either had to cut her guest list in half or give up one of her very favorite things to do in the entire world so the whole family could celebrate together.

Kathy was crushed. She felt so defeated, she told Robert, "I don't want to live here. This isn't good. We can't even have our family over for Christmas."

So much of her identity was tied up in being the person who brought everyone together every year. The memories were precious to her, and the prospect of making more of them was a big part of the holidays for her. It was a big part of what life was all about for her. Not being able to fill that role in the family, not being able to have everyone over like they always had, made her feel defeated.

And suddenly, her new life in the new house didn't feel so full of promise and possibility, or even peaceful.

As far as Kathy was concerned, it sucked.

Instead of being filled with holiday spirit, she was struggling with feelings of loss. And Robert began to experience some emotions of his own. He felt hurt. And also kind of offended. He snapped back at her, "Hey, I don't like living here either compared to what we used to have, but we agreed to do this, and all you do is complain that we can't host a Christmas party."

And just like that, Robert and Kathy started slipping back down the mountain.

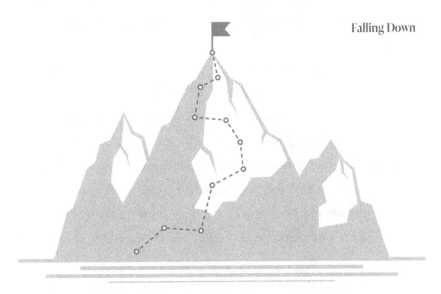

Falling Down

# You Are Here

Nobody stays on top of a mountain forever.

You're human; therefore, you're going to screw up. No matter how good you get at the habit of owning it, no matter how strong those muscles that keep you firmly planted in reality get, you are going to face challenges. And at some point, you are going to face a challenge you're not ready for. Maybe you'll have an off day, get tired, get lazy, be in a bad mood, whatever. Maybe the challenge will be so big, you won't feel like you have the tools you need to handle it (even though having made it this far, we're pretty sure you do).

Bottom line: when it comes to failure, it's not a question of if but when and how.

Think about the person with substance abuse issues who's sober for two years, faces a life challenge, and falls off the wagon. Or the person who, after following a strict budget for months, goes on a spending spree because, hey, it's Christmas! Or the person who quits going to the gym for a day, which turns into a week, which drags on for a month. It may not take that form in your life, but trust us—failure will happen. You're going to slip back down the mountain.

And that's okay.

One of the biggest parts of being accountable is acknowledging to yourself that you are not going to do this perfectly. That's what living in reality is all about. You're constantly going to be going through these motions where there's a push-pull. You're constantly tweaking and adjusting and self-correcting, and sometimes you won't make the correction until it's too late. Sometimes you won't make it at all.

So get ready for what may be the most important piece of advice in this book: *Don't worry about falling. Focus on what to do after you fall.*

When you fall, it's not permanent—unless you quit. As long as you treat a failure like a stopover on the journey of your life, it's just another part of the experience. Go back and figure out what happened and why, and then either alter your plan or just get back to executing it. It's that simple.

# Stopping the Slide

The reason it's so precarious at the top of the Accountability Mountain is that up at the summit, there's nothing left to attach yourself to if you slip. That's why you need to surround yourself with people who can lift you up when you fall. We're not talking about random people, like some of the people you left behind on the climb up. We're talking specifically about people who are up there with you on top of the mountain, working to stay in reality and maintain a life of accountability.

Salem learned this after he left Denver and moved to New Mexico. He was living in a town called Hobbs, which, to be honest, was kind of a dump, because that's where they tend to put nuclear enrichment facilities. And after about three years, it started to get to him. He started waking up in the morning feeling like *I'm in the middle of nowhere and it sucks, and is this what my life is going to be forever?* And he fell back into victim thinking, and once that started, he followed up with some victim behavior.

In other words, he started falling down the mountain.

Luckily, Salem had a partner in his supervisor,

*When you fall, it's not permanent—unless you quit. As long as you treat a failure like a stopover on the journey of your life, it's just another part of the experience.*

a guy named Randy. When Salem first got to New Mexico from Denver, Randy quickly demonstrated that he was the kind of person Salem could trust—he did what he said he would do, no excuses. So Salem was transparent with Randy about what he had been through in Denver and the changes he had committed to and the way he was going to live his life. He was open and transparent, and because of that, Randy became both a mentor and a friend. So when after about three years Salem started struggling and slipping back into some of his old patterns, Randy noticed. Not only did he notice; he said something. He took Salem into the office they shared and told him he seemed to be veering away from the plan he had shared with Randy a few years before.

He didn't say it in a judgmental way. He said it in a caring way, with radical candor. And when he finished pointing out what he had been seeing, he also said, "I'm here for you if you ever need anything."

That turned out to be the most important thing he said.

Salem didn't go to work that day expecting an intervention, and it wasn't exactly welcome. At first, he got defensive and denied there was a problem at all. But when he thought about the way Randy reached out, not as a boss or a supervisor but as a friend who cared, he realized his friend wanted the best for him. It turned out to be the wake-up call Salem needed. Being reminded of his plan and how his victim behavior was derailing it was enough to motivate Salem to recalibrate. He got back on his journey, did the things he needed to do, and within a year, he was selected to go to the UK for a new leadership role. And it might never have happened if he didn't tie himself to someone he could trust.

## The Upside of Failure

Failure doesn't necessarily mean your whole plan was wrong. However, it's a good indicator that something in your plan has to change. And there, in that recalibration, is an opportunity to make your plan better. Go through enough failures, and your plan will be absolutely bulletproof.

We know this because we both continually go through this process on everything. Staying at the top of the mountain requires constant adjusting and tweaking, so you remain victorious no matter what life throws at you. It's about sustaining—about keeping it going as a lifestyle—as opposed to doing it one time. Because if you don't sustain your progress once you've reached the peak, you've got nowhere to go but back down.

Think about the difference between a diet and a nutrition plan. A diet is a temporary thing—you restrict your calories dramatically for a while, you lose weight, you deem yourself "successful," which means the diet is over so you can go back to eating normally … and you gain the weight back. Sometimes even more. That's why diets fail. You haven't done the work to change the way you eat. If you're going to lose weight and maintain it, you need to find a new, healthier way of treating your body that becomes part of your life. You can't go to the gym, get in shape, and then stop going and expect to stay that way. You need to change how you think and how you do things every day.

But that's the great thing about diet and exercise plans, or any plans built around SMART goals. Not only can you leave and come back, you can modify them. If an aspect of the plan doesn't work for you, it doesn't mean you have to abandon the whole thing. You just tweak it. You keep what works and get rid of what doesn't and refine it and make it better. That's how a diet becomes a nutrition plan. You live with it long enough to tailor it to your needs, which includes accounting for failure.

If you define your success as being perfect, you will fail. But if you view success as a constant journey, you can get a lot of happiness just being on that journey, even when you slip and fall. Because slipping and falling is just another opportunity to adjust your plan and come back even stronger.

# Staying in the Zone

Since slipping off the mountain is inevitable, it helps to have a partner you can count on—not an "accountability partner," but a human who loves and cares about you and wants the best for you. The two of us do that for each other. We've each tied our rope to the other, so if one of us starts to slip, the other is there to throw his weight to the other side to keep him from falling all the way down.

However, whichever one of us falls still has to do the work to get back up. Nobody can do it for you.

Another thing that can help you stay near the top of the mountain is counting your blessings as opposed to your hardships. Salem has made this a daily challenge. He wakes up being thankful that he did, in fact, wake up. From there, he names three things out loud that he's thankful for. And he swears it really works as far as putting him in the right mindset to have a good, productive, joyful day.

Try it, and see what it does for you. As soon as you wake up, before you check your phone, name three things you're thankful for. Then at night, before you go to sleep, do the same thing. This isn't just a random exercise—there's actual science behind it. Your brain connects itself with things you're actually doing. If you get up in the morning thankful to be alive, thankful to have an opportunity to see people you care about, to do work you care about, it's like setting your intention for the day. Your brain starts the day knowing you're going to do those things. As opposed to waking up and thinking, *Oh, crap, I'm going to have to sit in traffic for an hour.* Or *That project is due, and I'm so far behind I'll never catch up.* It's the difference between starting your day as a victor or as a victim.

> *As soon as you wake up, before you check your phone, name three things you're thankful for. Then at night, before you go to sleep, do the same thing.*

You get to make that choice every day. So even if you screw up one day and let some victim behavior sneak in, you can reset your intentions before you go to sleep, when you remind yourself of three things you're thankful for before bed. Then you go to sleep feeling good and wake up with a new opportunity to have a victorious day.

# Accountability Partnership That Works

When you're living the life of a victor, you see opportunity in everything. Each one of those opportunities is a chance to climb even higher, to places you couldn't have imagined when you started this journey. But at the same time, each one can challenge you and possibly knock you back down. In other words, you need to be prepared for the rough spots, and the best way to do that is to make sure you're not on this journey alone.

Find someone you trust and invite that person to be radically transparent with you. Ask them to call you out when they see you slipping and promise to do the same for them. When you make that part of your plan, you're building in reinforcement to keep you from falling too far. If you slip into waiting and hoping, or giving up, or making excuses, or blaming, or not seeing reality at all, that person will see you and tell you. They can give you the support you need to recalibrate and get back on track.

Robert received this kind of help during the holidays, when he was having trouble supporting Kathy's struggle. There are three men he purposely invited into his life to support and challenge him. And they did that, especially the challenge part, when he poured his heart out about Kathy getting down about their new life and how frustrated it was making him feel. A lot of friends—typical, ordinary friends—would have agreed with Robert and maybe joined in and bashed her, or bashed their own wives. But Robert's friends did not do that. They said, "We know and love Kathy. We know she's an awesome wife. If she's hurting, you need to support her as you stay the course; you need to be humble and not discount her feelings." They cared enough to be honest with Robert, which helped keep him grounded, which in turn helped him understand his wife and work together to stay focused on their goal through a difficult time.

They helped Robert and Kathy stay on track and stay on top of the mountain.

If you're not willing to be called out and have somebody attached to you like that, not only could you fall down, but you might also stay down. That's why it's essential to have people in your life who are on this journey with you. When you attach yourself to other people who want to live this life with you, only want to see you be your best, and are willing to help you keep from falling back down where everybody else is, they help you stay on course.

They may not be able to "hold you accountable," but they can call out your BS—and sometimes, that's all you need.

## ACCOUNTABILITY EXERCISE: WHERE ARE YOU NOW?

Now that the journey is complete (but not over), go back to your Satisfaction Wheels. Look at how your numbers have changed from when you started this book to where you are today. Are there areas where you feel like your life has more joy? Are there areas where you feel inspired to do more, achieve more, be more? Don't look at those areas as failures—look at them as new opportunities. This is only the beginning. You get to decide where to go next.

That's the joy of accountability.

Is this making sense?

Are you seeing how this can help you

live the life you really want?

Tell others about our book.

Take a photo of the book cover and share on

your favorite social media.

Let them know how this is affecting you and

send them to get a copy for themselves at

**www.NobodyCaresBook.com**

# CONCLUSION

*Accountability breeds response-ability.*

—STEPHEN COVEY

Just by finishing this book, you've taken a huge step toward no longer living life as a victim. Because if you paid any attention at all, you'll never really be able to look at things exactly the same way. You've probably already caught yourself making an excuse, or saying you can't do something, or waiting and hoping, and thought, *OMG! They got me.*

Which is perfectly, completely normal. We both do that every day.

Owning it doesn't mean being perfect. It means being able to identify when you're being a victim so you can snap out of it. So that when you fall off the mountain, you can climb back up and remain victorious.

In case you forget, here's a quick reminder of where we've been:

We started at Obliviousness, where you weren't even aware that you were a victim or that there was a problem.

We moved to Blame, where you pegged the reason for your problem on someone or something else.

We climbed about a half an inch into Excuses, where you stopped deflecting responsibility for your problem onto someone else and instead came up with a reason for it.

We reached the point where you realized no one but you is responsible for your problem or dissatisfaction but decided it was too hard to solve it.

We climbed even higher to the point where you tried to solve your problem, but when you failed, you waited and hoped for something to change.

*Owning it doesn't mean being perfect. It means being able to identify when you're being a victim so you can snap out of it.*

Then you took the first step away from victimhood and crossed the ravine into victory by finally acknowledging the reality of your problem.

Instead of turning back from the ugliness of your problem, you embraced the suck and immersed yourself in it and accepted it as your reality.

Finally, accepting and understanding your problem enabled you to find solutions.

You "just did it" and enacted those solutions, and became fully accountable and fully victorious.

And you learned how to sustain your life as a victor, including what to do when you fall down.

In other words, not only have you reached the top of the mountain—you have the tools to climb all the other mountains on your journey.

Imagine what the world would be like if everyone climbed this mountain and pursued victory in their own life. A world without obliviousness, or blame, or excuses, where everyone is focused on living in reality and finding solutions to our problems, so those problems get solved and we keep climbing higher and getting closer to the ultimate peak. It would be amazing.

It's a big dream, we'll admit, but it's a lot of why we wrote this book. We don't care if we sell a million copies. But we really, really want this book to reach a million people.

Which brings us to our final exercise: Now that you've finished this book, don't put it on the shelf.

Give it away.

Or buy another copy so you can keep your notes.

The journey to accountability may start inside each of us, but as we've hopefully made clear, we all need other people to join us in the journey if we want to be our best.

So give this book to someone you know who is struggling, who needs some guidance and some help to find satisfaction in their own life. Give it to someone who is pursuing excellence and could use some extra support. Give it to someone you care about, who you want to experience the same joy and peace you've been experiencing. And when they're finished, encourage them to pass it on to somebody who they care about. So instead of being just a few random people who really, really care about accountability, this thing becomes a movement. And eventually, maybe the world can start to move toward victory and peace.

Whoever you are, if you're making this climb and you want to tie yourself to someone to make sure you keep moving up the mountain, whether you're struggling through a setback or just looking to become more accountable in your life, we'd love to hear about it. We've been where you are, and we'll be around, or someone else in the network will be, to help.

We'd love to hear from you.

So we've created a community where like-minded people—people who are on this journey and want to help others and get their support—can connect and share their stories.

You can find it at www.NobodyCaresBook.com.

By the way … "We Care!"

# CONTACT US

We'd love to connect with you and learn your story as you take more ownership for your life. Visit our website to find resources to help you on your journey: **www.NobodyCaresBook.com**.

Email us at **info@NobodyCaresBook.com** if you want us to bring this topic to your next team event.

Join the conversation on Facebook and LinkedIn and encourage others on their journey.

Look for us on Facebook and LinkedIn under Nobody Cares Book.

**Facebook**          **LinkedIn**

# ACKNOWLEDGMENTS

We fully acknowledge that we would have never completed this book without the amazing team at Advantage Media, and specifically Lisa Canfield. When we first met Lisa, we knew she was the one who would understand our passion to share these principles, and someone who could take our two voices and make the book read as one. She did it!

We are so thankful for her patience, focus, dedication, and creativity to bring all our thoughts, stories, and emotions into this book. Lisa: you are a Rock Star!

We also want to thank our friends at Renaissance Executive Forums who brought us together in the first place. Our CEO group has encouraged us and supported our efforts to make this passion a reality. True accountability is found in community, and our group lives this out.

# ABOUT THE AUTHORS

Salem Thyne is married to Soreya Thyne and is the father of four beautiful children: Gloria, Salem, Penelope, and Alex.

Robert Hunt is married to his beautiful wife, Kathy, and has two grown children, Lauren and James.

We are proud Texans who believe that it is more fun to give than to receive. We enjoy building teams, finding new opportunities, and helping the people God brings into our path.

CPSIA information can be obtained
at www.ICGtesting.com
Printed in the USA
JSHW031301200922
30752JS00003B/18